FINDING GOD IN ALCOHOLICS ANONYMOUS

FINDING GOD IN ALCOHOLICS ANONYMOUS

WHAT THE OLD—OLD TIMERS KNOW

MICHAEL

COPYRIGHT © 2009 BY MICHAEL.

LIBRARY OF CONGRESS CONTROL NUMBER: 2009911889
ISBN: HARDCOVER   978-1-4415-9880-6
                SOFTCOVER   978-1-4415-9879-0
                EBOOK   978-1-4415-9881-3

This book was printed in the United States of America.

To order additional copies of this book, contact:
Xlibris Corporation
1-888-795-4274
www.Xlibris.com
Orders@Xlibris.com
71642

CONTENTS

Special Thanks To:
Victory Family Church
Cranberry, Pennsylvania

INTRODUCTION

"I simply had to believe in a Spirit of the Universe, who knew neither time nor limitation. But that was as far as I had gone. With ministers, and the world religions, I parted right there. When they talked of a God personal to me, who was love, superhuman strength and direction, I became irritated and my mind snapped shut against such a theory. To Christ I conceded the certainty of a great man, not too closely followed by those who claimed Him. His moral teaching—most excellent. For myself, I had adopted those parts which seemed convenient and not too difficult; the rest I disregarded." (Big Book pg.10) (1)

"My people are destroyed for lack of knowledge, because thou hast rejected knowledge." (God—through Hosea 4:6)

"There is a principle which is a bar against all information, which is proof against all arguments and which can not fail to keep a man in everlasting ignorance—that principle is contempt prior to investigation." (Big Book—Wilson quoting Herbert Spencer 570)

Can you find the solution to life's problems if you take to heart the three passages above? Two are from the basic text of Alcoholics Anonymous (AA) known as the Big Book with the second quote coming from Old Testament Scripture found in the Bible. Do you think that this mind-set of rejecting thoughts explains why some people continue to struggle when they come into AA while others immediately turn their lives around becoming full of love, joy, peace, long suffering, gentleness, goodness, faith, meekness, and temperance?

The successful appear to have the world in the palm of their hands while others suffer in many ways after giving up the drink and continue to struggle for a manageable lifestyle, searching desperately. If we are honest, we have all been in this tough spot sometime during our sobriety. Most of us are somewhere in the middle. They label it "white-knuckle sobriety," always fighting just to be OK or accepting a mediocre life.

I always wondered if there was something more to becoming sober or maybe something I missed that the founders of AA knew that I could use as I trudged my road to happy destiny. Maybe there was some information that Bill Wilson could not share directly with us when he wrote the Big Book. After all, people would always tell me, "If you would just quit drinking, everything would be alright." Well, they lied.

In the same breath, I understand the addictive mind and the sensitive areas opened up as I address this subject. I want to provide some basic knowledge so that even if you do not agree with the findings, you will be well schooled to discuss these topics with others.

There are not too many opinions and thoughts, mostly anti-religion and anti-Christian, that I haven't held for myself at one time or another. I identified strongly, early on, with a third of the initial 100 members of AA who wanted nothing to do with religion and its theories. Many of the thoughts and beliefs that I held were based on what other people (i.e., preachers, ministers, mystics, rabbis, song writers, etc.) told me of God. I always rejected them without doing any research to validate or disprove what I was being taught.

After many hours of study, I can now pass on the findings that I have frantically searched to uncover and the new realities that are being revealed daily. I had many views about what the Bible did and did not say but never studied it with someone who was actually knowledgeable in Scripture or knew Jewish tradition and law. I have also come to believe that the Bible in and of itself, and *not any man*, is the only authority on God. If I come away thinking that God or the spiritually inspired writers of the Bible are harsh, present God as someone who "gets" you, contradict themselves or are someway in error, or if I feel condemnation after reading a verse, then it is me who does not understand what I am reading in relationship to the true biblical message of a Father-God who loves His children and it is up to me to ask God for clarification, and I will receive it.

I have provided many scriptures and verses so that you can follow up and prove the Word for yourself. The most accurate New Testament Bible translations, in my opinion, are the original King James, the Amplified, the American Standard and the Catholic Bible. The Catholic Bible is different mainly in the Old Testament books.

I have studied the history of AA in depth, and I do not believe many would be sober and alive today if the evangel's message were pushed hard during early recovery. I am grateful that God inspired Wilson to speak in spiritual terms instead of religious tones to the alcoholic.

The word *evangelist* finds its root in the word *evangel* which literally means "preacher of the good news" (Strong 2099). If you ever hear anything preached that is not good news, it does not come from God. You may call it what it is, bad or dark news. God is total light and at all times good (1 Jn 1:5). The early pioneers knew of the evangelistic message, and this is where we find relief for the sober alcoholic who still suffers needlessly. It is explained here in later chapters.

My desire and prayer are that you will keep an open mind and test or prove what I am saying. Prove all things; hold fast that which is good (1 Thes 5:21). I bind and remove any blinders that keep the truth from you. As Jesus said in John 8:32, "And ye shall know the truth, and the truth shall make you free." See how it will affect your life and change your thinking patterns. Seek God as Wilson so appropriately said when he wrote "that God could and would if He were sought."

For easy reference, many Bible passages that are not printed in the text can be found after the end notes at the back of this book.

I

ALCOHOLICS ANONYMOUS AND RELIGION

I imagine Bill Wilson struggled terribly as he authored the Big Book of Alcoholics Anonymous, trying desperately to meet the needs of the spiritually minded and those open to God, while addressing the concerns of the person who is angry and scoffs at prayer and calls himself an atheist or agnostic. It must have been a very difficult balance to strike.

His conclusion was to guide us as best he could without forcing any religious convictions or denominational doctrines onto the suffering alcoholic. He didn't want to offend anyone, and he knew that alcoholics could not be forced and must be led. This is why the slogan "Let AA save the alcoholic's butt, and let religion save their soul" is often quoted. They have always tried to win the man rather than the argument.

Wilson dealt with a two-edge sword. Does he write pointedly about the power and the strength that will completely free us in all areas of our lives, above and beyond the drink problem, or does he soft-pedal God and get us sober long enough to open the door so we may find the way to God?

AA does not want to be a religion or denomination exclusive to the recovering alcoholic. It does not want to be Christian or Jew or Muslim or any other religious sect. Religious entities sometimes find this offensive because new AA members often will not talk about God or Christ or any firm religious standard. People outside the program sometimes forget the depths of religious resentment that has built up in individuals and society as a whole over the years. Inside church, we often refer to this as religious rot. If someone opened a church called "The Non-Religious Church of God," the place would be packed.

Successful churches today are those that walk the talk of God's love and love for one another.

If you were to take a hard look inside AA you will rarely see someone with long-term sobriety who is not spirituality minded and God focused. If he or she does exist, he/she is usually miserable with much hurt in the heart.

AA's primary purpose is to help alcoholics achieve sobriety, and the main thrust of the Big Book is to help the alcoholic find a power greater than himself that will solve his problem (Big Book 45). It gives the person in recovery the choice just as God gives us the choice. God tells us to choose life or death (Deut 30:19). The Big Book stresses that the member must become a spiritual individual, which is what many religions try to teach their members. AA members also believe that sobriety is contingent upon the daily maintenance of their spiritual condition (Big Book 85). Being spiritual is key.

Wilson and Smith

I can see Wilson, talking the matter over with Dr. Silkworth (2) or the Reverend Sam Shoemaker (3), seeking advice as to how he could carry the message of the evangelistic Oxford Group that would place the alcoholic on the path to physical, spiritual and emotional healing. Actually, Wilson was probably belly aching as to why his approach and the need for a spiritual conversion were not working. Wilson, in New York, tried pushing a dramatic spiritual conversion from his sobriety date in November 1934 until he met Doctor Bob in May 1935. He found God-thumping did not work. Not one person became sober during these six months. It was not until Dr. Silkworth told him to lie off of the God stuff and talk about the effects of alcohol that progress was made. This was when he met Dr. Bob.

Reverend Shoemaker played an equally important part when he told Bill to give the new alcoholic a small piece of God—just crack the door a little—and then trust God to bring him or her to where He (God) needed him or her to be (Knippel 116).

Robert Smith, AA's cofounder, is lovingly referred to as Dr. Bob in the rooms. He was a proctologist from Akron who was known as the town drunk. Dr. Bob was a very spiritual man who belonged to the Oxford Group for more than two years before he met Bill, yet being full of God and fundamentalist Christian values, Smith could not stay sober.

This is an extremely keen observation. Wilson having gone through a spiritual conversion could not help anyone become sober; however in trying to help other alcoholics, he himself stayed sober. Smith, who was not trying to help others but was full of God, could not stay sober. It was not until the man side in Wilson met the God side in Smith that sobriety began to take hold for both, and AA was founded. This brings home a very strong point that we know from biblical teachings. When the supernatural (God) and the natural (man) meet, things happen. It takes both. God could make everyone sober, but He does not. He will not override free will.

Higher Power

You often hear members refer to a higher power in the rooms. This phrase is used only twice in the first 164 pages of the Big Book. It is used to: 1) soft-pedal God to the new person while allowing him to make a choice as to what he will believe, and 2) it eliminates any controversy that might arise from someone pushing his or her religious beliefs on another.

Someone once told a new member that he could use a tree as a higher power. That stuck in oral tradition. It gives relief to the newcomer for any prejudice he might have against religion, and it also cracks the door to a power that is truly greater than himself. Most people believe in God, but they do not like religion. In time, though, some wise soul will grab a toothpick and tell the new member that this is what they have done to his higher power, the tree, but only when he's ready to accept it.

It is amazing how Wilson interwove biblical principals throughout the Big Book in a very subtle and pragmatically effective way that alcoholics can grasp. Most alcoholics do not know that they have been spoon-fed many spiritual principals found in the Bible.

Members often incorrectly state that the basic text of the Big Book was written out of the epistle of James. This is not correct. It is true that early members did study this letter and that several great concepts are taken from James. At one time they had even considered calling AA the James Group. These misconceptions are due to many publications pertaining to AA and the Oxford Group being written by individuals who do not have the training and working knowledge of the Bible and without this information they do not see the influences of the Bible throughout AA. References in the Big Book's text are found throughout the Old and New Testaments more than they are limited to James.

For example, William James, the author of "Varieties of Religious Experience", was also read by early members in New York. This has probably caused further confusion with the epistle of James. Along with Shoemaker's Oxford Group teachings, Emmett Fox, who was an author and public speaker was also a main influence in early AA. Fox was a theologian who preached the Word out of the Bible in its entirety, giving Wilson a good deal of spiritual background.

The Oxford Group

The Oxford Group has deep roots in Alcoholics Anonymous. It was founded by Frank Buchman, a minister from Pennsylvania. Buchman had a falling-out with the elders of his church and, full of anger and resentment, left for England. In 1908, he heard a woman by the name of Jessie Penn-Lewis proclaim the Gospel message. She was a study of the great Charles Finney who is known as the greatest leading evangelist in the United States, starting in the early 1800s. D. L. Moody, another great evangelist, also influenced Buchman and Shoemaker's Oxford Group with his teachings (Barger 135).

Full of love and forgiveness, Buchman returned to the States and started a 1st Century Christian Fellowship group whose purpose was to carry the evangelistic message in small settings known as home groups. These people would then infiltrate the message to the church. In 1926 it became known as the Oxford Group, named after Oxford, England, and was renamed in 1941 to Moral Re-Armament. There is still one group in existence today.

Through a series of coincidences, it was Wilson's attendance at the Oxford Group in New York and Dr. Bob's participation in the Akron, Ohio Group that brought the two together. Wilson, six months sober, went to Akron on a business deal that fell through and was in need of a drink. Instead of drinking, he was connected to Reverend Tunks who was said to be the only preacher in town who cooperated with the Oxford Group that had begun there in 1928. Wilson was eventually introduced to Dr. Bob, stayed in his home for roughly three months, and AA was founded.

The evangelistic message was strong in Akron AA, and they appeared to be more God conscious than those in New York. Dr. Bob became sober on June 10, 1935, and from then until his death on November 16, 1950, he helped sober an estimated 4,800 drunks. Bill Wilson made a statement once that Dr. Bob was more effective than he was in helping the alcoholic become sober (Dick B. 5). It is what Dr. Bob knew that resulted in 75 percent of these members becoming sober, whereas in New York the member struggled. In 1938, through a study completed by the Rockefeller Foundation, it was estimated that there were 110 people sober in AA, with 70 members hailing from the Akron area.

II

SPIRIT, SOUL AND BODY

There is something to people intuitively knowing, to a point, what God is and what He is not. God tells us that He has placed inside each of us what is right and what is wrong and that He has revealed Himself to us (Romans 1:18-20). So when someone says something that doesn't align with our heart, we know it and balk. Wilson said the same thing. He tells us that deep down inside each of us lies a Great Reality (Big Book 55), and he's talking about God.

This is also the reason that many of us are extremely critical of ourselves when we make a mistake. We learned in recovery that all the mistakes we make are the result of a spiritual illness and that we are not 100 percent spiritually fit. If we were, we would never miss it. Before we learned this, we were judge, jury and executioner on ourselves. We already held court and did not need anyone else to punish us. We were held accountable in and by the sin itself. Thank God we do not punish ourselves anymore and can be loving and gentle.

The Bible teaches that we are made in God's image and likeness (Gen 1:26). Because God is spirit, we are too. We are a three-part being. We are a spirit, we have a soul (which is our will, mind and emotions) and we live in a body.

> "And the very God of peace sanctify you wholly; and I pray God your whole *spirit* and *soul* and *body* be preserved blameless unto the coming of our Lord Jesus Christ." (1 Thes 5:23)

Our earth suit (body) stays here when we die, and our spirit and soul go with us.

Take a moment and look at someone whom you would consider a role model and see if there are these two common traits present: True, balanced leaders are very spiritual people, and spiritual people are not led by their emotions.

If you are not spiritual or spiritually led, you are what the Bible calls *carnal*. Carnal means you are led by your natural physical senses of touch, smell, hear, taste and sight. Carnal people are emotional and physical creatures instead of spiritual beings. Spiritually led people are rooted in who they are *in* God and are not driven by fears, hurts and emotional disturbances.

The great news is that we can have our minds renewed and become spiritual creations that are not emotionally driven. Emotions for us are no longer crises, and we no longer need to react at every whim of our feelings. The spiritual person tells his soul (will, mind, emotions) and body what to do instead of the soul telling the body and spirit (sometimes called our heart) what to do. Smith Wigglesworth said it best. He stated, "I don't ask my body or my mind how I'm doing. I tell it how I'm doing."

III

LIMITING GOD

We instinctively know when someone is truly acting out of love toward us or just putting on a show. God operates in love, and we are made in His image; therefore, we operate in love. Call it a heightened awareness or sensitivity. We know deep inside that some of the theology and religious beliefs taught to us just do not sit right, and we are unsure where to find the truth. Unfortunately, many of us stop there as we allow the religious beliefs of others to dictate our thinking and limit us from the light of God. We build a fortress that makes it difficult, if not impossible, for God to reach us and for others to teach us the many truths that will transform our lives. We keep them out, and we lock us in.

For instance, God is not a respecter of persons (Acts 10:34, Rom 2:11, Col 3:25) and always minds His own business. God neither favors one person over another nor does He push where He is not wanted. He is always a gentleman. He does not differentiate between you and me. We are all His children, and He wants the best for each and every one of us and constantly seeks a way to connect. That's why He is the Father-God. He's a father first.

He does not get one person sober and another He does not. You hear it said, "I don't know why God chose me to become sober but didn't help so and so." He chooses us all to be sober. This places the responsibility solely onto us, but with His help. He can not pick and choose, if He did, He would be going against His word. God does not interfere with man's will unless He is asked. Anything above that would make Him a selective God. If God picked you to be sober and blessed and poor Johnny was stuck with addiction, sickness, and poverty why would Johnny fight against God's will? Why trouble yourself with going to the doctor if that's what God wants for you? Be sick! Give up trying!

Quit working, and live in poverty! God willed that and you do not want to oppose God, right? Sounds crazy, doesn't it?

God simply cannot reach us unless we create and open a path for Him and the only way to do this is through prayer and asking. That's why the famous prayer "God, Help Me" is so effective. When it's said, we have usually tried everything we know and completely surrendered, and this allows God to enter.

I hear you saying, Hold on now! God can do anything! He can do everything, but He won't. First of all, God cannot lie. If He lied just once, we could never believe anything He said. Secondly, His Word, tells us that He has given us all dominion and power here on earth and in heaven except over the will of others (Eph 1:19, Luke 10:19, Mt 16:19, Ps 115:16, Col 2:9-10, Mt 28:18, Gal 2:20, 1 Cor 2:5). Look up these scriptures in your Bible (or at the end of this paper) and see how they read. Because He has given dominion and power to us, He will not do what we can do. He will help but not do it for us.

Sovereign God

So if God were in total control of everything, we would not have free will to choose because He would actually be controlling our lives. We know that we have free will because we chose to believe what we want to believe and act how we want to act.

Peter tells us that it is God's will that none of us should perish (2 Pet 3:9). If it is His will and He does control everything here on earth no one would perish. People do perish and because they do, it must not be up to God. The only one left is us, or He's not telling the truth. We decide how and what to believe.

It reminds me of a story about a man who was happily married for 50 years. When asked why he was so happy, he said, when living with someone you have the choice to be either happy or right, and I choose to be happy.

I can choose to go through life believing that there is a loving God who wants to take care of me and live my life to its fullest and die to find out that I was right. If I was wrong, it will not matter because I will be dead and gone. Or I can choose to go through life on my own, *not* believing in God or His promises, and when I die, again I will verify the truth. If I was wrong, I short-changed my life here on earth. If I was right, it does not matter because I am not going to know it. In other words, we must choose. The truth exists outside of us, and we have no influence over it.

The root controversy with this idea of a sovereign God comes from the word we often use to describe God. We say He is the *sovereign* God. This term *sovereign* is not found in the Bible. There are ten other names that God calls himself, and not one of them is *controller*. If we are using the 13th-century word as defined by Webster, God does qualify as the supreme authority or ultimate power. Unfortunately, most people believe that this word means supreme controller of everything, and this is not accurate. He is not a control freak. He is not filled with fear as we humans sometimes are and driven to control. He could manage us if He wanted to, but again, He has chosen not to.

The God Side and the Man Side

When it comes specifically to drinking, alcoholics have an understanding that others do not. We appreciate why someone would get tight when he is already in trouble. We value the trials of becoming and staying sober. After a period, we learn that a drink never makes any negative or positive situation better. We understand that in war it is easier to maintain our position on a hill than it is to take the hill. Staying sober is a lot easier than becoming sober—that's if you get another opportunity.

We all must quit drinking at some point. Some of us try to quit before we get to AA, others quit when we get to AA, and the remaining "plug the jug" after we are here for a season. Some of us stop when we give up the ghost. We will eventually quit! We choose when.

The Big Book tells us that people like the effect alcohol produces (Big Book xxvi Dr. Silkworth's letter). We would look for the solution to our woes in the bottle, trying to source a consistent power and strength that we could rely. We made a poor choice and believed in alcohol. Today we choose to trust in God and life rather than fear and death.

I personally struggled for many years, sober, and never quite got it. I never obtained the peace that surpasses all understanding that others speak of and the promises found that are a result of "working the program" (Big Book 83). On a scale from one to ten, the strength I had to overcome my problems was rated around a three or four. As far as not drinking I am a perfect ten. I had not drunk alcohol for a long period. This wasn't enough. I still had to breathe and live. I wanted "the power" to overcome all of my problems, but I restricted myself to using the power only to not drink. We are taught that alcoholism is only a symptom. I proved that. I was not drinking, and frankly, I knew that there was more to life than trudging any happy road to any happy place. I saw people living full, healthy, productive and prosperous lives and I wanted it too.

My friends, seeing my struggles, would tell me that just because I sit in a chicken coop doesn't make me a chicken anymore than sitting in an AA meeting or attending church makes me a useful member of society. I had to change how I was doing things, but I could not. I longed for that internal peace. No matter how hard I tried or how much I read and gained book smarts, true rest never came for any great duration of time. Personal knowledge didn't do it.

Reading and studying the Big Book of *Alcoholics Anonymous* and the *Twelve and Twelve* was not enough to bring *me* complete freedom and release from the bondage of fear, hurt and depression. Maybe it is for you. I thank God for you. I just did not have the strength that I needed to overcome all of my problems. It was freeing to some extent and I have been placed in a position of neutrality as far as alcohol is concerned, and today I have no opinion on alcohol. If I'm tempted, I recoil from it like I would a hot flame (Big Book 84). I could quote paragraphs from the text; tell you all about Doctor Bob, Bill Wilson, Ebby and the other old-timers. We could discuss why it is necessary to work the 10th step (continuing to take daily inventory and promptly admit our mistakes) out of the *Twelve and Twelve* rather than the Big Book and eliminate the notion of those who have not studied and say that they need to redo their 4th step of taking a personal inventory. No, you do it once and live in the maintenance steps (steps 10 through 12), correcting and processing new issues that come up and then talk to someone when necessary as in the 5th step and forgive, forgive, forgive.

I know the history of AA in depth. All of these things brought temporary relief, but something was still missing. *I was relying on man and myself* instead of taking the direction that Wilson actually told me in the Big Book to take. I did not fully rely on God.

My actions screamed, "God, you handle my booze problem, and I'll ruin the rest of my life". Half-measures availed me nothing. I had limited God from working as much as He could in my life. Ephesians says best regarding how we control the power working through us.

> "Now to Him (God) who, by (in consequence of) the (action of His) power that is at work within us, who is able to (*carry out His purpose through us* and) do superabundantly, far over and above all that we (dare) ask or think (infinitely beyond our highest prayers, desires, thoughts, hopes or dreams)." (Eph 3:20 Amplified)

So how do I come to know more completely a God whom I can trust and permit to work through me? This was exactly why I was so full of fear. I trusted in myself when I knew that I did not have what it takes, and it generated more and more fear. Not only that, but I tired doing everything myself.

IV

WHAT THE OLD-TIMERS HAD

I believed in God. Well, if the truth were known, I identified strongly with Wilson who could never quite buy into the fact that God loved him personally when there was always such a great void between them. Wilson had a tough time in sobriety for a period. I, too, was worried about what others were doing as I found it difficult to swallow and understand the claims of some people who had a God. Not that it was any of my business. And for Christ . . . well . . . . a great moral code . . . some good ideas . . . probably OK for a big brother . . . . but a God who actually loved and wanted me?

Driving myself to find out why an estimated 75 percent of the AA pioneers stayed sober and why they repeatedly told us that God had restored them to their right mind started a search into what I had passed over or missed. Fifty-eight times in the first 164 pages of the Big Book, some derivative of the word *recover* is used. This revelation created a curiosity in me as to why this emphasis is centered on the fact that the early members, between 1935 and 1939, say they recovered or were healed or a miracle took place, and yet many members today are petrified to say they too are healed of alcoholism. I wanted more out of life than just giving up the booze.

Recovered or healed, I knew that I did not want the old me back because I believed that my mind never was quite right. I needed something new, not improved. I needed transformed, not restored.

It was in this quest for relief that I actually looked hard at the Oxford Group and the early AA program of recovery. This is where I found my answer. It was right in front of me the whole time. Thank God.

It is in this seeking of God and knowledge of Him that I want to share. Wilson told us to do this. Like some, my religious thoughts were the ones that I had heard some others preach. There was no attraction. I had beaten myself enough since childhood and was not giving someone else permission to pound me. After all, who were they to tell me! I knew I was a sinner. I had strange behaviors. I intuitively understood what the Bible teaches about me being a spirit, soul and body. My spirit would be disgusted at times with my thinking and actions.

Usually I found that my abnormal behaviors were driven by hurts that I had no knowledge of or thought I had successfully buried. You did not do the things I did or act in the ways I acted and be called a stand-up guy. I always fell short of how or what I thought I was or how I should act or be. Sober or drunk, there was little difference. My breath was better, except now I was cursed into remembering everything. Then at times, it felt as if others thought they could make their candle brighter by blowing out mine. I guess in their spiritual sickness, they never realized that by lighting my candle the darkness in my life had no choice but to go. I have since learned to always put something in people and not take it out.

I am not sure where I formulated my ideas about whom and what I am, now that I know, in part, of whom God says I am. I see that those former beliefs were not established in truth. I knew my deeds. People telling me I was going to hell did not do much for my morale either. Try sending someone to Hades when he already lives there. Never has reprimanding me been an effective tool in turning my life around. Only love is. Love motivates me, and this is exactly how God corrects us—through love.

> "Or are you (so blind as to) trifle with and presume upon and despise and underestimate the wealth of His kindness and forbearance and long suffering patience? Are you unmindful or actually ignorant (of the fact) that *God's kindness is intended to lead you to repent* (to change your mind and inner man to accept God's will)". (Rom 2:4 Amp, emphasis added)

God continues loving me until change comes about in the same way the old-timers loved me until I changed. God knows my true heart, the true me who wants to be all that God wants me to be.

Love of a Sponsor, Love of God

This is exactly why the program works so well. No sponsor, no program. It's not a mystery. We naturally pass it on from generation to generation, Christ's new commandment to love one another (1 John 4:21) and the attitude that I'll take care of you and your kids if you take care of me and mine is a driving force in the rooms. Most members do not even realize that they are practicing Jesus' commandment to love one another. We are responsible. Whenever someone reaches out for help we want the hand of AA to be there, and for that, I am responsible. It was freely given to us, and we freely give sobriety to others. Oh, how some churches familiar with AA long for the love, camaraderie and the fellowship that we have in our rooms. The old guys of the program loved me. The old and beautiful gals were gentle. They loved me until the confusion lifted and I could start loving others as they had taught. No one can touch an alcoholic like another alcoholic. No one can touch other people except through love. We are to seek charity (love) first (1 Cor 13:1)—a gift God reserved for people in ministering to others. People say alcoholics do it to themselves. Probably, but does it really matter? We do most things to ourselves. Satan kicks you when you are down. People who love help you up.

We owe much to those who have tried to love us, understand us and help us as they walked away feeling used, confused and somewhat bewildered. They did not understand. We did not understand. Thank God for their trying. We are always grateful for and to them because we might not have stayed alive long enough to get sober if it were not for their love and tearful tolerances.

This love from AA members who helped us is the beginning of recognizing that God really loves us and wants us to love Him in return. In Genesis, God says, "Let us make man in our image and likeness," and in Revelations, He says that He made us for His pleasure (Rev 4:11). We please Him like our children please us. Our nature is love. God needs us, and He treats us as He would treat Himself. He knows what it is like to be alone. God knows the separation that addiction causes. He has given the sober drunk's imperfect love to light the way for another with the perfect love that casts out all fear (1 John 4:18). Thank you God!

V

FAITH

One of the most loving truths learned was from my sponsor who always told me to have faith. We are healed by God's grace through faith (Ephesians 2:8-9). I am not where I want to be, but thank God I left where I was. Thankfully, He will meet us wherever we are regardless of any circumstance we find ourselves in. He met me while working through an obedient catholic priest who liked to cuss and in my truck driving sponsor who could not quote the tenth chapter of Romans but walked and talked it. He spoke to me continuously about faith and showed it through his actions.

> "So then faith cometh by hearing, and hearing the word of God."
> (Romans 10:17)

So how do we hear about faith in AA? Of equal importance is how we learn more about God in the rooms. Faith begins only where the will of God is known. You cannot believe or trust God in an area where you do not know what His will is. How do we come to completely know of a God who loves us so much that He would actually make a path for us that will bring us closer to Him and then place us in a position where we find His grace to be sufficient for our shortcomings and all life's events?

> "My grace is sufficient for you." (2 Corinthians 12:19)

and

"For I know the thoughts and plans that I have for you, says the Lord, thoughts and plans for your welfare and peace and not for evil, to give you hope in your final outcome." (Jeremiah 29:11, Amp)

We have faith not to drink. We learn it by hearing the stories of others who are sober. The common theme heard is: 1) It got so bad that I asked God for help. This is the favorite and most effective prayer of a drunk: God, Help Me. Simple and to the point, 2) I developed a faith wherein I could stay sober because I saw you staying sober, and if a drunk like you could do it, maybe I could too. 3) I looked and saw how God was working in your life and hoped that He would work in mine too. Now that is AA faith.

It is a good faith, a beginning or rudimentary faith and one that we need to expand if we want to go further and find the real power that Wilson talks about—who will solve all of our problems and take us beyond not drinking.

The Oxford Group's Faith

The early 100 members of AA, before the Big Book's publication in 1939, had another faith source. This was before the program was mapped out and made available via the book. They had Bible faith. In the beginning, Rowland, Ebby, Dr. Bob and then Bill were all part of the Oxford Group movement. They attended and had strong ties to this fellowship until Wilson's initial breaking away in New York in 1937, followed by Clarence Snyder of Cleveland, Ohio, in 1939 (4). Wilson and his alcoholics thought they were special and should be treated accordingly with their own separate meetings. Its crazy how even after a season of recovery, some still think we're special.

Catholic drunks in both New York and Ohio were not permitted to make a public confession (lead or testimony) in the Oxford Group meetings; therefore, they could not become sober "in" the movement (Kurtz 68). These were the main reasons they initially broke free from this fundamentalist group, resulting in the small group meetings we know today. The Oxford Group was also incorrectly labeled as Nazi sympathizers during the late 1930s, which added to the need for a complete breakaway so as to not taint AA's name.

Becoming sober in this fundamentalist Christian group had many benefits. They practiced the Christianity that was experienced before the Bible was canonized and when the letters known as epistles and the four books of the

Gospel were being written. These writings were authored between 48 and late 90 A.D. This season of time was a highly spiritual period.

The initial members studied the Bible and *meditated* (meaning to murmur or repeat to oneself) on its teachings. Worry is the negative form of meditation. We lack study as a group inside the rooms today. Their meetings mainly consisted of a pre-selected member sharing his experience, strength and hope with whom the new person would identify strongly, followed by prayer. Other nights they would have a Bible study. Someone was always selected to open and then close in a prayer of his own words. Jesus warns us against using vain repetitions (Mt 6:7).

When was the last time we prayed the Ephesians prayers (Eph 1:17-23 and 3:14-21) at an AA meeting (5)? Do we understand that whenever two believers agree on earth for something in prayer, it will come to pass? Would this generate a greater desire to start praying together? This is why a husband and wife's prayer is so effective. Have we discussed Matthew 5 (6)? When did we pray during the entire meeting? Have any of us studied Jesus's last words in John 13 through 16 (7)? You will find peace there. How about being filled and led by the Holy Spirit (8)? The early members did these things and more religiously.

Other than the Lord's Prayer or the Serenity Prayer few formal prayer sessions take place today. The old adage of those who pray together stay together holds much truth. And, folks, praying when you get up and when you go to bed doesn't represent the constant communion the early church had or what Wilson had in mind in the 11th step when he tells us to improve our conscious contact with God. I'm not saying this critically as much as to make us aware that we should pray more, study biblical truths more and talk less.

Wilson was asked once via a letter from an active AA member in Pittsburgh, Pennsylvania, about Bible study. Here is his answer:

"There is no reason why a group of AA's shouldn't get together for Bible study; no reason at all why a group of AA's in a church should not associate themselves into a sort of spiritual kindergarten fellowship, into which anyone might be invited. As a matter of fact I am anxious to see this sort of thing tried." (Knippel 83)

Dealing with a Drunk

Bill Wilson, armed with Bible knowledge and an alcoholic himself, was very sensitive and afraid to be too pushy with God, knowing how some drunks would react. He had tried this approach, and everyone he worked with stayed drunk. This direct approach was the result of Wilson's own spiritual experience or "hot flash" (Big Book 13) (9) and the alcoholic's need for a spiritual conversion (10). He initially thought this dramatic spiritual conversion was the only way to sobriety. Unfortunately, Bible thumping to a *new* person was ineffective. Alcoholics must be led and not pushed. Thank God you are no longer new, and your mind is open to new ideas.

The Oxford Group in Akron, moreso than the Oxford Group's Alcoholic Squadron in New York, were quite the followers of the Bible, specifically the New Testament. Prayer and meditation, morning readings, prayer meetings, waiting on God for guidance and fellowship in the spirit were common Akron occurrences. They talked God more than they talked booze. They carried the Gospel message verbally and through their actions, while being respectful of other beliefs and generally minding their own business.

Dr. Bob, more effective in dealing with the new guy, had a revelation of grace that Wilson appears to have struggled to receive. It is my opinion, that even though Wilson had a spiritual understanding to some point, he never really understood the principal that we are saved by grace through faith (Eph 2:8). Wilson never appears to have been relieved of the guilt that disappears once we have truly surrendered in step 3. Several letters Wilson wrote contain the theme of looking for grace rather than already having received it (Knippel 77). This conflicts with the true Gospel message that you *are* saved by grace if you only believe.

Paul, who authored roughly two thirds of the New Testament, had this same battle with his brother Jew during his time on earth. This question of, "Is it grace or works that get you into heaven?" is what the epistles of Galatians and Romans are all about. The New Testament conclusion is that it is grace and grace alone that saves. In other words, we can never be good enough and would eventually fall short if left to our own devices.

This is a good example for us because we have both extremes of development in sobriety. We can identify with Wilson who struggled and was depressed for many years into sobriety, never believing in grace, and Smith who was reasonably peaceful and accepting of life.

As members, we are not trained, for the most part, on God issues other than the miracles of fact that we continually see take place in the rooms and through any self-study. Wilson and Smith were trained minimally through the Oxford Group on God issues. This is why Wilson, with Bob's urging, instructs us repeatedly to seek God and return to the denomination of our choice. They knew their message would fall short in helping us. If we could only listen to and do as Wilson advised, then God can do His best for us. We limit God's best for us through our ignorance and the strongholds of our unhealthy beliefs.

In writing the original manuscript of the Big Book and reviewing its contents in Bill Wilson's kitchen, the initial New York AA group suggested at one point that they omit God entirely from the book. This was not because they did not believe in God but they did not want to offend the newcomer. They were also battling the public explosion of a recovery program for alcoholics that demanded fulfilling requests from a variety of people with varying religious backgrounds as they tried to meet the needs of the masses.

Finding it difficult to discuss Christian views without hindering recovery to the agnostic, Jew or other religious orientation is a treacherous task. In a sense, writing the Big Book actually eliminated the one-on-one witnessing of a loving God when viewed in the context of needing to get recovery out quickly to those desperately in need. They had to trust God to those whom they could not personally witness to.

Thank God for Lois Wilson, Bill's wife, who literally tossed everyone from their house except Bill and then demanded to know "to whom Bill and the others truly owed their sobriety and life" (Wilson—CD). To no one's surprise, Bill conceded and immediately made the necessary corrections to include God in the original text and in writing of the *Twelve Steps and Traditions*.

Can you imagine Alcoholics Anonymous without any God? It was better for Wilson to leave a God to our own understanding than be responsible for the millions across the world who would never have found recovery from a seemingly hopeless state of mind and body by proclaiming his God as the only way or omitting God entirely. Different sects of Christians cannot agree on the cross and what we receive as a result of Jesus's death at Calvary let alone the confusion caused by bringing a variety of religious beliefs into the rooms. How would a bunch of opinionated ex-drunks who are Bible illiterates know how to overcome this? This is another example of God meeting or providing for us wherever we are.

For those outside of the rooms who do not know that AA does indeed focus on God, look at this fact. The word *God* is use 131 times in the main text of the Big Book compared to the phrase *higher power* which is used twice. God is obviously the more important. AA would be just another short-lived self-help group if we had no God to receive the power from. We desperately need something outside of ourselves to guide us. Some of us think we are God only to find that He has better ideas. After all, our best thinking is what got us in this mess to begin with. We all owe our sobriety to God, being coworkers with him.

The text is consistently dropping hints and guiding us back to rely on God as we discover Him. We are told in the fifth chapter of the Big Book:

    (a)   That we were alcoholic and could not manage our own lives

    (b)   That no human power could have relieved our alcoholism and

    (c)   That God could and would if He were sought" (Big Book 60).

We are also told to be quick to see where religious people are right and to make use of what they offer (Big Book 87). So it is up to us to seek and continue seeking regardless of how much we learn until we find the depths of a loving, gentle, patient, helpful, counseling, comforting, strengthening, long-suffering, and reliable Father and Son, who are available when we search for them. We are always open to what He shall show us next.

VI

SEEKING RECOVERY

There is and was much consideration in expanding the early member four-step approach into the 12 steps we now know (Snyder CD, Wilson CD) (12). When we continue to practice step 11 and "seek through prayer and meditation to improve our conscious contact with God as we understood Him, praying only for knowledge of His will for us and the power to carry that out," will we grow, be made whole and complete and lack nothing. This is what the Bible calls the abundant life or in the Greek, the word is translated to the *zoe* life. Those who do not continually seek seem to peak out and do not get better. We can become placid after getting over the initial crisis of not drinking and rest too long on our laurels being happy with the progress to date. That will last for a season or two, but it's easier to study and prepare when we are not in dire straits and are more open to suggestions. Troubles will come. Why worry and wait? Be prepared!

So how do I get well spiritually or develop my spirit? Where can I find the healing power of God that has no limits? How do I know the full extent of God and the spiritual world?

God is so big that it takes time to know His complete love. The way you learn about God and His will for us is how Wilson instructed—through seeking and then more seeking. You are searching now by reading this book. I know that God will show you more than what you think. He always does. His word says:

> "Call to me and I will answer you and show you great and mighty things, fenced in and hidden, which you do not know (do not distinguish and recognize, have knowledge of and understand)." (Jer 33:3 Amp)

Throughout this book, I hope many things for you. My biggest prayer is that we stop limiting God and His best for us. I hope you receive the revelation and your personal rhema that God *is* all light and there is no darkness in Him. He constantly yearns for our attention. He is always in our corner, cheering us on! If we could only see where religious people are right.

The Lepers

There is an interesting story told in the gospel of Luke. Luke was a physician who traveled extensively with Paul. In this parable, he speaks directly to us about the results that we can achieve depending on what level we seek and have faith in God.

> "And it came to pass, as he (Jesus) went to Jerusalem, that he passed through the midst of Samaria and Galilee. And as he entered into a certain village, there met him ten men that were lepers that stood afar off: And they lifted up their voices, and said, Jesus, Master, have mercy on us. And when he saw them, he said unto them, Go shew yourselves unto the priests. And it came to pass, as they went, they were *cleansed*." (Luke 17:11-14)

Leprosy is a disease that physically eats away at your flesh. These lepers were probably missing pieces of their bodies and were confined to a colony. Sounds like some of us in AA—these Samaritan lepers were outcasts too. Jesus healed them all and they were made *clean*, meaning that the leprosy no longer was consuming their flesh and their sickness was arrested. We are made *clean* in AA when we quit drinking and work the 12 steps to recovery. To continue:

> "And one of them, when he saw that he was healed, turned back, and with a loud voice glorified God. And fell down on his face at his feet, giving him thanks: and he was a Samaritan. And Jesus answering said, were there not ten cleansed? But where are the nine? There are not found that returned to give glory to God, save this stranger." (Luke 17:15-18)

How many people are healed of their alcoholism and you wonder where they went? I thought ten were healed? Only one came back? But look at what happens next to those who quit drinking and take it a step further.

"And he said to him, Get up and go on your way. Your faith (your trust and confidence that spring from your belief in God) has made thee whole." (Luke 17:19 Amp)

Because this one leper came back and believed, he was made whole or complete. His faith made him whole. Remember, lepers have parts of their bodies missing. Well, not this leper. He was restored and made complete, lacking nothing because he believed. And if God can do this with physical ailments, He can do it in all areas of our lives.

In this passage, it talks nowhere about what the leper's faith is except when Jesus said, "Your faith has made you whole." What action did the leper take that demonstrated his faith in God for his healing? The action he had taken was believing he was healed and coming back to thank God.

Now contrast this to what we hear repeatedly in the rooms. People always say that they are *always* asking God to keep them from drinking. After a person is somewhat grounded in their sobriety, what would occur if he or she thanked God every day for his or her sobriety instead of asking or begging? What if you forget to ask each morning? Would you drink? Is God's healing only good for one day? Personally, I haven't asked in more than 20 years, though I thank Him continuously for all things.

By the way, in the Bible the word *ask* does not mean to beg. It is generally defined as demanding something that is due. So again, we need to know God's will if we are going to demand.

Does this leper need to ask daily? No, his action of faith, not his asking, is what made him whole or complete. The asking cleaned him. He asked once and then thanked and praised God for doing it.

Even when tempted, you can either ask God to take the thought away or thank and praise Him for removing it a season ago. Which is more effective? Read Hebrews 12:6 to clarify this point for yourself. There is only one thing that pleases God.

VII

EARLY STEPS IN RECOVERY

The first step for Bill Wilson and Dr. Bob in sobering the alcoholic was to qualify the person. The question to be answered dealt with if you *honestly* wanted to quit drinking. They would determine if the candidate met the following requirements: a) being a drunk and b) if he or she was really done drinking. If he or she was they helped you. If not alcoholic or were what they called a mental defect (how can you tell the difference?) or if he or she still wanted to drink, they would move onto someone who was whipped. It is the booze's job, not man's, to convince us that we're beat.

If you fit the criteria, after a soul searching session with your sponsor, you got down on your knees and accepted the salvation message. This was step 2 and known as surrendering in the Oxford Group. In effect, surrendering makes the watered-down version of step 3 written in 12-step programs today not nearly as effective as it could be. Of course, you need the true understanding that empowers, which was verbalized back then from one member to another and especially from the sponsor. This step made you completely right with God. Wilson had gone through this same step when Ebby brought the message to Bill (Big Book 13).

The next phase was making relationships right with others, or our amends steps of 8 and 9 today. Finally, moving forward in helping another alcoholic become sober which is the current step 12.

Three of those four steps were expanded and carried over into the steps we now practice (found on page 75). The honesty part of wanting to quit drinking was omitted because it is too confusing to determine if anyone actually has an honest desire to quit drinking. We never openly qualify anyone today. Many people have the honest desire to quit hurting, but giving up the drink forever is another story. That's why we do it one day at a time (2 Cor 4:16, Mat 6:34). Today you need to only want to quit drinking. Now in step 1, "We admit that we are powerless over alcohol and that our lives have become unmanageable," is taken as a point of self-admission.

After the publishing of the Big Book, the 3rd changed from a surrender and confession that Christ is our Lord and Savior to, "Making a decision to turn our will and our lives over to the care of God as we understood him."

Do not get nervous about confessing anything until you understand the what and whys that were spoken. With some sobriety and God experience and after reading the introduction, you are curious as to what the original members knew that we do not share today. We are no longer prejudiced about God and religion. You, who are sober for a while, can now handle it. Besides, if God scares you off, booze will scare you back in—that's if you get another chance.

It's a quick test to see to what extent you have the working power of God in your life. This should also be a new standard as to how well your program is working. Don't fall under condemnation with this either!

Are you still full of fear? Do you worry? Are you emotionally balanced or are feelings a crisis? Any drama queens or kings? Spend hours on the couch? Do you pay your bills on time? Is there anyone whom you harbor ill feelings against? Watch porn? Is there still anger in your life? What or whom do you resent? Are you jealous and insecure? What about sex? Do you over eat? Can't eat? Can't sleep? Do you work too hard? Have you gossiped lately? Have you or do you create strife in your home, workplace or home group? Steal from work? Are you a street angel and house devil? Holding any grudges or unforgiveness? And the list goes on. These issues are open to any one of us as soon as our feet hit the floor in the morning, and they reflect our true spiritual or heart condition. No one is above any of these behaviors. We all have clay feet. We only hold God in high esteem.

How much of each day do you give to prayer and reading the Bible? Do you read any spiritual books? Whom did you help today, this week, this month? Is your faith strong when in a crisis? What would your spouse, kids and sponsor say about you? When was the last time you made coffee for or cleaned up after a meeting?

Is your life working for you, and do you get up praising God even in the middle of a mess? James tells us to count it all joy (James 1:2). Are God's grace and living in His blessings sufficient for you? Have you learned that it's better to live in the blessings (Deut 28:1-15) than desire a miracle?

I'm not condemning nor am I being critical. I am trying to point out that we all have areas in our lives that need work, and who better to mold and guide us then the One who created us? No one knows you better. If we look hard, we see that the behaviors and thoughts that hinder us are the things we do not want in our lives anyway.

AA people, for the most part, are not preachers or teachers or evangelists or of the five-fold ministry of the Gospel. Nor does God want us to be. We can all study, though, and have a stronger God-centered foundation for living. How can we help others if we haven't studied ourselves and do not know what God's will is for us? God's will is mainly found through the Bible and the inner witness speaking to you that always aligns Himself with the Bible. So the question now becomes, "Do you know His will for your life, and does it align with the Bible?"

The reason for explaining this news to you is an obligation that I have to God, to you and any brother on earth. I believe it's what God wants me to do. He had, unbeknownst to me, been placing me in positions to receive this knowledge. He has probably done it for you too. In the reading of the Big Book and the Bible, many revelations and truths are exposed. These gifts are given to anyone who asks for them. Here's a great Bible passage:

> "If any of you lack wisdom, let him ask of God, that giveth to all men
> liberally, and upbraideth not; and it shall be given him." (James 1:5)

Solomon in the Bible is thought to be the richest man to have ever lived. He is known for asking God for wisdom and knowledge. What wisdom and knowledge do you need? What wisdom are we to learn from the Oxford Group and early recovery? What was lost, and what did they know that we don't know? What did they find so appealing or compelling that drove them to their knees to accept the Gospel message? Why were they not afraid to boldly state that they were restored or made whole?

The answer is that they heard who God is and what He provides for us in the suffering of His Son on the cross. For faith comes from hearing the word of God. The amount of faith we have is contingent upon how much we hear of God and His will for us. Little hearing, little faith! Much hearing, much faith! Early members talked about and read the Bible continuously. So the question now becomes, "at what point do we become disparate enough to openly seek and hear the message?"

There are two fundamental gifts that we receive when accepting the message. One is that we are placed in a right standing with God, and the other is that we become a new creation.

VIII

RIGHT STANDING AND RIGHTEOUSNESS

Be quick to see where religious people are right. Make use of what they offer. (Big Book 87)

Here lies an interesting truth. We can conclude with a great deal of certainty that the original 100 members of Alcoholics Anonymous did not practice the exact 12 step recovery program that those who came after the publishing of the Big Book *Alcoholic Anonymous*. Thank God for His wisdom and Wilson's obedience that we were bottle-fed the milk of spiritual growth. The pioneers were taught a strong foundation as to who and what they were in God, and this generated a higher recovery rate.

Not being provided the biblical side of God generated some false truths that hurt us individually and as a collective whole. Let me explain how it personally affected me.

I've always wanted to be a stand-up guy. I never could do it on my own strength and willpower. I always wanted to overcome these defects and shortcomings (the Bible refers to sins as shortcomings) in my character and I never could. I always wanted to be someone who loved and trusted God and my brother. I always wanted to be one of God's chosen, and I never was. The problem was I did not have the wisdom, knowledge and power.

Today I am in right standing and I am righteous with God, and no one can take it from me. I have what the old timers had, and I will always be in right standing and God will always find me righteous. Now that, my friend, is a BOLD statement. It's not because *I earned* the place or position. It wasn't because I am *good* enough meaning neither my good works nor my lack of bad works got me there, and neither will yours get you there. It wasn't because I was bad enough either. Being bad won't keep me out of my right standing with God. I wasn't one of His angels. I'm still not. I am one of His saints or set-apart ones. You can be too. It has nothing to do with who I am, who I am not, or what I am other than the fact that God sought and loved me first. My *not* being in right standing had everything to do with me being separated from God.

Separation from God

At one time Jesus was separated from God. Jesus, God's anointed son, doing the work His Father wanted him to do was apart from God. He was dying on the cross when He cried out, "Eli, Eli, lama sabachthani?" That is to say, "My God, my God, why hast thou forsaken me?" (Mat 27:46). God literally had to turn His back or turn away from Jesus as He was dying on the cross because all of the sins and transgressions of this world, mine and yours—from all the ages that are and were to come—were placed upon Christ when He was crucified.

Now we know about sin and people turning from us. Not one of us has ever gotten away with anything we did. We know about being punished in and by the sin itself. We are experts at sin.

My brother is a sinner. He shoots archery competitively. Every time he lets an arrow fly and it does not hit the bull's eye, he sins. He misses the mark.

Jesus, however, is the spotless Son, without blemish who never missed the mark (2 Cor 5:21). God, who is so pure and holy, cannot be in the presence of darkness (sin) and this is why He had turned away from His Son (Isa 59:2). Imagine being at the lowest point in your life, crying out for help to your dad, and your dad turning from you! God had no choice! When we are in the throes of addiction we place people in the same position that God was placed.

The sin and transgressions of all people, whoever was or will be, were so dark that God had to turn away. It is the sin that separates us from God and brings forth spiritual death while not allowing us to stand in God's presence.

God in His infinite knowledge, wisdom and love had to find a way to remove the sin consciousness of this kingdom so that He could come to us and be with us. He longs for communion with us. God made man. He made us in His image and likeness. Then God made woman.

> "And the Lord God said, it is not good that the man should be *alone*; I will make him a help meet for him." (Genesis 2:18 emphasis added)

Notice that God first made man and immediately came to the position that it was not good for Adam to be alone. Who better than AA members to understand the anguish of loneliness? How would God, though already knowing everything, know that it was not good for Adam to be by himself? The answer is that God knows what it is like to be alone.

Sin separates God from man. So God sought the world for a person—Mary, the mother of Jesus—who was obedient and pure to bear His spotless child. He, in turn, gave up His Son to die on the cross so the sin barrier could be removed and our sins cleansed. There must be a sin substitute or payment to remove the wall or casm that separates God from us, and Jesus was it. He paid the sin penalty.

S

GOD   **I**   **YOU**

N

Sin is the divider. God has permanently erased the dividing wall by sacrificing His Son on the cross and placing all of our transgressions and sins upon Jesus. God is no longer removed or alienated from us, and we can now come freely or boldly to Him. There is now peace on earth and goodwill toward man.

Not only did He remove our sins and separation, He also took away all of our infirmities, weaknesses and diseases, and we *were* healed and made whole, complete and lacking nothing.

> "And thus He fulfilled what was spoken by Isaiah, He himself took our weaknesses and infirmities and bore away our diseases." (Matthew 8:17)

Now that is the Good news of the Gospel! He has already done it for us. Completely! Our barrier is gone. We can now go boldly to God. It's not atonement or covering of the sin but a thorough cleansing or removing of sin, sickness, disease, weakness and infirmities. We are made whole and complete in Him. Now when God looks at us He sees us as only pure beings in Christ. This is the great mystery that Paul continually speaks of that is hidden from natural man.

I equate it to someone who has a $20.00 bill in his pocket but does not know it. That person can be starving to death and eating from a dumpster because he's not aware of the money. Many people are unaware of what Jesus accomplished and are eating out of dumpsters when they could be having steak.

Just because we do not see it or understand it does not mean that it is not true or real. Take electricity, for example. You cannot see an electron. We are told that it is the flow of these electrons that causes a light to illuminate. I have never seen an electron and the scientist could be telling a story, for all I know. I do know that when I take the action and turn the light switch on, the bulb lights. *I believe* that when I flick the switch, the light will come on or I would not have flicked the switch. You could say that I have faith in the switch and electricity. From experience, I know the will of the light switch.

I have faith that the chair I sit in will hold me. I see a chair and I know that it is for sitting, so I sit. I believe that it is in good shape and I believe that the person who assembled it knew what they were doing. The chair holding me will prove my faith or that I believed correctly.

The Jews have a great grasp of this concept. They do not have a Hebrew word like we do for *faith*. They don't believe. They *know* what God said and what He will do. That's what great faith is—when you know that you know that you know. Here's another example of how our thinking can limit us.

I take a common everyday red apple and slice a piece horizontally at about the thickness of an average human hair. If I showed you this sliver, more than likely you would have no idea what it is or was and you can even see it. Just because you do not know what it is does not make it any less of an apple. Many things exist beyond our scope to understand or identify with our physical or carnal senses.

So allow me to ask you? What sins and sicknesses of yours and mine did Christ die for when He removed the barrier that kept us from God? Did He die for those we commit today, those from yesterday or the ones in the future? And when are you forgiven—2,000 years ago or today, or when you ask?

He covered them all 2,000 years ago—past, present and future. Now that's good news. The almost too-good-to-be-true news, and it gets better than that. Sins are removed, and I can now boldly go to God with all my needs. I am in right standing with God. You and I are no longer separated from His light.

Maybe you believe that you have some sin that is so ugly that God would never forgive you. Maybe it is ugly. Maybe it's not as bad as you think. I can tell you one important thing. You have already suffered long enough, and Christ, the Anointed One, has paid the penalty of sin and you can be in right standing with the Father right now. You can be forgiven and righteous according to God. Thank God.

All degrees of sin are the same to God because all sin closes us off from His light. There is not a *worse* sin to God, nor is there a best sin. They are all worse. They all separate us. Besides, who wants to be the best sinner who gets to heaven?

> "For whosoever keeps the law (as a) whole but stumbles and offends in one single instance has become guilty of (breaking) all of it." (James 2:10 Amp)

I'm always trying to stump God! I'll ask Him, "Hey, Dad, what was my last sin?" He looks at me with a funny grin, shrugs His shoulders and replies, "I don't know kid." That's because He doesn't remember. He chooses not to remember on purpose. He wants nothing to come between Him and us. When I get to heaven one of my favorite past times is going to be watching people come before God with the $20.00 in their pocket and the long list of excuses and failures and mistakes, rehearsing the whys and whats of the things they've done, saying, "when He says this, I'll say that," and so on and so forth. I will sit there with Him and smile, knowing it's a done deal if only they believed when they asked.

I want to watch their responses and the reactions that He gives them. I can see God changing the subject or ignoring the issue completely and simply stating, "My silly child, I love you and have absolutely no clue as to what you are talking about."

See what the B-I-B-L-E says, He says:

> "I, even I, am he that blotteth out thy transgressions *for mine own sake*, and will not remember thy sins." (Isaiah 43:25 emphasis added)

> Or

> "As far as the east is from the west, so far hath he removed our transgressions from us." (Psalms 103:12)

It is important to realize that when you travel directionally from the north to the south, you will eventually start traveling north again. When you travel from the east to the west, however, you always travel east and *never* go west. Here are some other scriptures.

> "For I will be merciful to their unrighteousness, and their sins and their iniquities will I remember no more." (Hebrew 8:12)

Or

"And their sins and iniquities will I remember no more." (Hebrew 10:17)

Or

" . . . Know the Lord: for they shall all know me, from the least of them to the greatest of them, saith the Lord: for I will forgive their iniquities, and I will remember their sin no more." (Jeremiah 31:34)

Or

"I write unto you, little children, because your sins are forgiven you for his names sake." (1 John 2:12)

The last verse is a good one. Not because of who I am or what I have done but for His name's sake. His grace is what frees me. This is the good news of the New Testament. What a deal, and it gets better yet. Because the sin barrier has been removed, we are now placed in right standing with God or as the Bible states it, we are righteous. How great that our salvation has absolutely nothing to do with our own actions or lack of actions other than our asking Him into our lives and believing what He has done for us! His prudence knew what and who we are and how we act and think, and He has removed anything that will burden our fellowship.

GOD/ME

In Right Standing

SIN

If God came to me at this very moment and asked me, "Michael, what did you do that makes you righteous and makes you think you can be in my presence?" The only answer I could give Him is, "I did nothing, God, other than to believe that I am in right standing and this is only because you love me so much that Jesus died on the cross for me." Anything more than this is a works mentality, and the only work I need to do is believe what Christ has done. I cannot earn it.

And it gets better. Isn't it something that when we drink it gets worser and worser (legal grammar if you keep drinking) and when we make Jesus our Lord, it gets better and better? Once we ask Christ into our lives and acknowledge that He is our Lord and Savior, our spirit is sealed. We cannot take the decision back. Our righteousness is guaranteed. God knows our hearts. He hears our cries at night. God understands how our mind at times will conflict and deny our hearts with the battling in our mind over what we believe. He understands how we work and life's struggles. He made us. That's why He sealed us the second we gave our life to Him. It's a done deal. Once you are in, you are in. So those in AA who continuously say, "I had to redo the 3rd step," are not in agreement with what Jesus says. Once you are sealed you are sealed. You do it once, and that's it.

> "Labour not for the meat which perisheth, but for that meat which endureth unto everlasting life, which the Son of man shall give unto you: *for him hath God the Father sealed."* (John 6:27—emphasis added)

So whom will you believe? What the Bible states or some other? Look up these passages. They all convey the same message: 2 Timothy 2:19, Ephesians 4:30, Ephesians 1:13 and 2 Corinthians 1:22.

Good Bible doctrine requires us to always have at least two different witnesses (writers) to confirm the Word. Here you have Jesus who said it, Paul (or Saul) and the Apostle John who was Jesus's cousin. Earlier, I gave you five witnesses who say that God will remember your sin no more.

Yet some are still skeptic of this Gospel message. They don't believe that it is this easy or think that they can now go and sin and not be held accountable. They say the message cannot be true. "You just gave me a license to do whatever I want." Not true. Paul would say in today's vernacular, "Are you nuts"? He was asked this same question three times in the letter to the Romans. Why would anyone in their right mind want to go and get themselves back into trouble once they have been totally absolved?

It is difficult for guilt-driven people to understand that **what we do is not who we are!** The real you is your heart or spirit man. You would not be disgusted with yourself if your soul (carnal being) were in charge. You would probably like your actions. The behavior of the physical man and thinking patterns of the soul will only act appropriately to the degree that we listen to and are in commune with our regenerated spirit. God sees you in your spirit that was sealed when you gave your life to Christ. This is why we are told repeatedly to renew our mind (to match the spirit man and all its deposits) and that we can have the mind of Christ.

We also know that it is not the Holy Spirit or God or Jesus or the angels or satan that convicts you of wrongdoing. They either cannot or will not. ***God does not condemn you, and He doesn't allow others to either.*** It is your heart and your heart alone that convicts you when you are not doing what you believe you need to be doing.

> "For if our heart condemns us, God is greater than our heart, and knoweth all things. Beloved, if our heart condemns us not, then have we confidence towards God." (1 John 3:20-21)

God knows all things. He knows your hurts and heart issues. He sees us trying repeatedly to come to Him, and He knows when we miss it. I perceived Him one time in my spirit say to me, "Thanks, Michael, for not giving up on me." Can you imagine that God loves us so much that He would thank us for continually striving to reach Him and not giving up? That is someone who loves you.

It *is* this easy, and we cannot go on continually sinning. Maybe for a season or two but not forever. Once we turn our life over to God, we are no longer under the law of sin. Moses was given the law so that we are made aware of what we are doing. This is similar to how a red traffic light makes us aware of when to stop. Jesus has fulfilled the law. No law, no awareness. God now writes His law in our hearts, and we cannot habitually practice sin. He gave us a new heart.

> "A new heart will I also give you, and a new spirit will I put in you: and I will take away the stony heart out of your flesh, and I will give you a new heart of flesh." (Ezekial 36:26)

And because of this new heart, this occurs:

> "We know (absolutely) that anyone born of God does not (deliberately and knowingly) practice committing sin, but the One Who was begotten of God carefully watches over and protects him (Christ's divine presence within him preserves him against evil) and the wicked one does not lay hold (get a grip) on him or touch (him)." (1 John 5:18, Amp)

Now that doesn't say that you can't sin. What it says is that you cannot deliberately and knowingly practice anything that separates you from God.

Our flesh is weak, God knows it. As a matter of fact once you receive the revelation in your heart of how much God loves you, you begin to cry out like Jesus did on the cross the moment you perceive separation from God. No not for a second do we want to be removed from under His umbrella. Read Psalms 91 if you want to see how protected you really are: "A thousand may fall at your side, and ten thousand at your right hand, but it shall not come near you . . . . Oh the grace given to a wretched soul like me . . . . We can only be a spectator!"

And if we do sin and miss it, there is no big deal. Don't condemn yourself because that is not God's best for you. You are allowing satan to distract you. Immediately acknowledge what you did and move on.

> "If we *confess* our sins, he is faithful and just to forgive us our sins, and
> to cleanse us from all unrighteousness." (John 1:9 emphasis added)

That sounds like step 10. Along with forgiving and forgetting our sins and transgressions, the sealing of our spirits, being placed in a right standing with God, giving us the zoe life, we are also a new creation. The old you no longer exists. People tell me repeatedly about my past, and I tell them I have no idea who they are talking about. The old me has past. The new me is here. I don't live in the past, and I will not permit you to pull me there. I'm not being arrogant, and I have made amends where I have wronged others. God says I'm forgiven and that I am new, and I will go with what He says I am. Thank you, God.

> "Therefore if any man be in Christ, he is a new creature: old things are
> past away; behold, all things are become new." (2 Corinthians 5:17)

This means that the old you who continually drank, or maybe slipped time after time or after some period of sobriety, or maybe never really become sober or makes the same old dumb mistake once sober, is a new creature when you give your life to Christ. You are now brand new, and if you're new, then there is no past to feel condemned about, or ashamed of. The bottom line is that if you are in right standing and alright with God then you are in right standing. PERIOD.

Are there consequences for your behaviors? Absolutely! Both good and bad behaviors have consequences. You either put into your life or you take out. But the negative consequences are not from God. He doesn't "allow" them or "cause" them to come about to teach us a lesson. He can't. Causing us grief is of darkness. God is all light and there is no darkness in Him at all. Remember, He corrects us through love, just like the old AA guys who love you after you make mistakes.

> "This then is the message which we have heard of him, and declare unto you, that God *is light*, and in him is *no darkness* at all." (1 John 1:5)

Will you need to make amends? Yep. We want to be in right standing with everyone, as we do not shirk any of our responsibilities. God (like your sponsor) will even go with you when you make things right. And if you don't? You're still righteous with God, but your neighbors might not feel the same.

Ask for forgiveness of those you have harmed, acknowledge it to God and move on. Ask Him for strength, wisdom and understanding. Please, Please, Please, do not burden yourself and place yourself back under the sin by beating yourself up and actually giving the power back to the sin. God already removed the sin and you became righteous when you initially asked for and believed in your forgiveness. The only way anyone of us will not sin anymore is to not breathe. Although John says it is possible to not sin (1 Jn 2:1), that might not be an option right now so keep striving to be holy with the renewing of your mind through Christ Jesus.

Now let me take some time and digress here. The decision I am going to ask you to make next was the most difficult decision that I ever made had I not known what Jesus came here to do and what Jesus really says:

> "And this is the Father's (God's) will which hath sent me (Jesus Christ), that of all which he hath given me *I should lose nothing, ...*" (John 6:39 emphasis added)

So God's will for Jesus, according to Jesus, is that *He does not lose one of us*. That means you and me. We are precious to Him.

I came to Alcoholics Anonymous at age 21 and did not believe God wanted anything to do with me. To make matters worse, I was very angry, hurt and afraid. I did not want to be 20 years sober and still confused. Thank God I've grown and am healed. Thank God, too, that many of you are not separated from God like I was. Well maybe you were; separation is separation. Sin is sin and sin separates the non-believer. Jesus might have had me as his friend but I would not have believed it.

"Henceforth I call you not servants; for the servant knoweth not what his lord doeth: *but I have called you friends*; for all things I have heard of my Father I have made known unto you." (John 15:15 emphasis added)

I understand how this can be a difficult decision. The pain in my heart was from a very young age. I thought God *took* my mother and father when they were only 45. I had five other siblings. We were all kids ourselves and not ready for it. It was too painful for the extended family to come around us kids except for a grandmother and one uncle. Growing up I was hammered by Sunday school teachers who were junior trainees of Adolph Hitler. I had fingers pointing in my face telling me I was evil and of the devil when drinking. I was probably worth 50 of satan's imps! This is why the devil wants many of us back in his kingdom. We caused so much strife. Loving Christians prayed right in front of me, unsolicited, to cast out the devil in me. And that was when I was sober! I just could not understand why a loving God didn't intervene and answer my prayers. I never asked to be born. The Bible says to ask, and I asked. I'm not complaining, I'm just telling you my experiences.

I can understand not wanting to trust God. If you do not trust Him, ask Him to help you. He knows anyway why you do not trust Him. Ask for His wisdom. He must give it to you because He said He would.

You will come to understand that God and Jesus have very little to do with any of this. God only loves us and wants us to allow Him to do His best for us. I see His sadness because we do not welcome His help in the same way our children do not allow us to help. That's one of the reasons you are reading this right now: He has led you.

I have studied very hard to make sure that I impart these fundamental truths to you about Christ and what He has accomplished for us. We do not get them in their entirety in AA because God directed Wilson to get the booze out of us first. Thank God. Jesus dying on the cross for our sins is the foundation and cornerstone of what God can and will do for us. It is just the tip of the iceberg. There are so many more benefits we reap being the King's kids. I don't want to be misleading, so I've placed ample Bible verses in the back of the book for you to look up on your own. Everything you need to make an informed decision is present. I have held back no reason for not taking this step. There are no shortcuts and no reasons not to.

So tell me. If you died today, right now, do you know and are you confident without any uncertainty that you will go to heaven? There is a heaven, and there is a hell. Do you want a new life now? Have you taken step 3 as the original members have and not a condensed version? Do you want to be completely and totally free, a new creation here on earth, your past wiped away and forgotten, all your sins removed and you being made completely whole, healed and sealed? Maybe you have been away from God for a season and you need to be in right standing. I only want the best for you. You'll never be good enough to earn it. Going to church won't do it. Attending meetings and sponsoring many people won't do it. There is only one requirement: to believe that Christ died for your sins and confessing it with your mouth. If you want this grace in your life, pray this prayer out loud as I have already prayed it for you.

> **"Heavenly Father, you sent Jesus into this world so that He would not lose one of us. I believe that Jesus is my Savior and my Lord, and I thank you that He has taken away all of my sins when He died on the cross, overcoming sin, death, sickness, and poverty. He rose again and is now seated at your right hand. Thank you for planting your law in my heart as I go about your bidding. Guide and direct my life Lord as a loving Father would his son and as you see fit. I receive my salvation now. In Jesus's name, Amen!"**

Thank you, Lord! There is one more thing I ask you to do. Remember today. Write today's date and keep it close as a reminder that you have given your life to God through Jesus Christ. It's a big step and life is easier if you know Him. Continue to seek and I guarantee that this will be the most important and freeing decision you will ever make.

Carry this message to your new person, as you see fit, and bring him/her into a right standing with God. Explain the surrender step of the program as Dr. Bob did when he spent four to six hours individually talking to the 4,800 patients he treated after he became sober. Please do not let others struggle as we have. Thank you for being faithful and obedient to your inner calling.

IX

FORGIVENESS AND FORGETTING

"I'll forgive him, but I'm not forgetting!" You are probably hard on yourself too. Or we take the other approach where we can understand someone else making mistakes but can't see us being spiritually sick. We have been taught that it's good to forgive but we don't need to forget. Well that might be true for some, but it's not God's best. We are to forgive and forget as God forgives and forgets.

> "I, even I, am he that blotteth out thy transgressions *for mine own sake*, and will not remember thy sins". (Isaiah 43:25)

Why? There are two main reasons. The first is that you shut yourself off from the light. Any darkness you harbor, even if you are right, is still darkness, and we need (require, depend upon, demand, seek) the light. We have all had experiences when it is difficult to be in the presence of someone who has harmed you, even if you have forgiven them. The only solution is to forget. People tell me all the time that they cannot forget offenses. They do not truthfully say, "I choose not to forget," as if there is some alien powers making them remember. I know it hurts—both you and them.

Jewish tradition has a great way of forgiving. They say, "Father, I forgive so and so for doing this and that. Father, I forgive so and so for not doing this and that. Father, I forgive so and so for hurting me in ways that he and I are not even aware of, and by forgiving him, I release any and all bindings that bond me to that pain. Amen (so be it)."

We forgive in faith. Really, all forgiveness is done in faith. It is not something you physically see or touch. When have you ever seen a sin removed

50

or touched a cleansed sin? You may feel relieved of the sin but that comes only after you believe you have been forgiven.

If the feeling of unforgiveness returns, we take a stand and say, "No, I will not get back into that condemnation. I have already forgiven him and only want the best for him." Sometimes we do it through gritted teeth. When a feeling is no longer serving its purpose, it then becomes neurotic and can be disregarded immediately. If you have forgiven, you know it's forgiven and you're not a cow so there is no good reason to chew it twice.

I believe the main reason unforgiveness keeps resurfacing after we forgive is because of the devil, the author of confusion (1 Corinthians 14:33), who likes to cause strife as often as he can to keep us distracted from the conscience presence of God. The more he can keep your focus on some person, place or situation, rather than God, the happier he is. Being excessively busy with work, kids, sports, and meetings is his goal. Satan doesn't even care about you or me; he just hates God that much. The good news is that darkness cannot stay where light is. Turn on the light, darkness goes. Spread the love. Light someone's candle. Dive headfirst into helping a newcomer as Wilson suggests. Jesus tells us:

> "The thief cometh not, but for to steal, and to kill, and to destroy: I
> am come that they might have life and that they might have it more
> abundantly." (John 10:10)

The thief (the devil in Jesus's words) comes to kill, steal and destroy. He also tells us:

> "The sower soweth the word . . . (15) but when they have heard, satan
> cometh immediately and taketh away the word that was sown in their
> hearts." (John 4: 14-15)

The word, that you the sower sow, in this case is forgiving someone who has harmed you. Jesus tells us that satan comes immediately and takes, or steals, the word from your heart. So here is what occurs: You forgive somebody and two days later you start again to feel this resentment when the thought returns. He—being satan—comes and steals the peace you had when you forgave. This is satan distracting you and trying to have his way. Well it won't work. You know that you forgave the person. Praise God. You must have forgiven him or her or the filthy one would not be trying to *steal* the peace you received when you forgave them. If you did not have it then he could not steal it! He cannot take something you do not have. Tell God, "Thank you that I have forgiven so and so and bless him repeatedly for my sake." As a matter of fact, you will start laughing at the evil one because you are wise to the evil one's ways. Jesus just told us how the filthy imp operates. Don't permit satan to get his foot in the door.

A battle is going on in your mind that was already settled in your heart. The thought you had to forgive is from God. It is good, it is light and you do it. You may have a cunning or dark thought that the person is unforgivable. You cannot control any thought that comes into your mind. You can only evaluate and decide which ones you will allow to camp there. Take captive those that do not add value to your life.

I never worry about someone who says he or she struggles with doing the right thing or trying to do the right thing. It is the same for new people who seriously struggle, talking about wanting to drink. They never do. It's the ones who are sneaky that drink. Being aware of the conflict is an indicator that you have God's love in your heart and the imp is trying to steal your peace or mislead you. People who do not struggle are traveling in the same direction as the nasty one. You never run head-on into someone when you both are traveling the same way.

Carl Jung was a psychiatrist who treated Rowland Hazzard in 1931. He never knew his impact on AA and the significant role he played in the foundational truth that we must have a spiritual conversion in order to overcome our drinking and, I'll add, our life issues. Wilson found out right before Jung passed on that Jung actually thought the disease we fight was a spiritual battle being fought between evil forces and our spirits. Jung essentially did not want to bring light to what he thought was a sensitive area of the spirit world because people would think he was a little odd and eliminate his ability to help others (Barger 12). You cannot blame him as many people believe incorrectly that evil forces do not exist and rather believe that people are evil in and by themselves.

Another reason we forgive is if we do not forgive we are actually saying that what God did for us in having his Son die on the cross wasn't enough. We place our sins, however great they are in our mind, above Jesus's blood when He was wounded for our transgressions and bruised for our iniquities (Isa 53:5). It mitigates the whole purpose of him dying for our salvation and reverts right standing with God back to your good works and lack of bad deeds.

Now if you missed it, acknowledge it. Do not start prosecuting yourself. Simply say, "I missed it, Father," and move on. It's in the past. You do not even need to ask for forgiveness because when you accepted Him, all of your sins, past, present and future were forgiven. You do need to simply confess and turn from it.

"There is therefore now no condemnation to them which are in Christ
Jesus who walk not after the flesh, but after the Spirit." (Rom 8:1)

X

LIVING IN THE PRESENT

I always hurt when I see people living in the past. It's the compassion of the Holy Spirit working in love that tells me to carry the message to others. How does anyone still live in what occurred some five or twenty years ago? The answer is that they need to. It is serving a purpose. They see no other way. We all have different strongholds in life.

It reminds me of when I would speak at the local state mental hospital. People there are filled with anger, resentment and bitterness. Patients would tell me what occurred in their childhood as if it were yesterday. What a bond the prince of darkness has. They can recall only past hurts. We who have given our lives to God ought not to live in the past, and we do this by forgiving ourselves and others. We usually have trouble forgiving others when we hold onto and do not forgive our part in it. There is usually some sliver of truth about us that we are afraid to face.

Similar behaviors can be found in bees, buzzards and elephants. They operate on what they believe to be correct; their truth is not true either.

Did you know that if you placed a bee in a conical container with a sealed bottom and open top the bee would burn itself out looking for an opening and eventually die because he believes the only way out is through the bottom?

Or place a buzzard in an 8' x 6' box with no roof and the bird will eventually die of starvation because, even though it can fly mighty distances, it will not fly or jump out. It can see only the walls.

The elephant is the best example. When elephants are babies, they are tethered tightly to a pole in the ground that they cannot move. When full grown, they are tied with a light stake that is pushed by hand into the earth. They were taught as babies that they could not move the pole so as soon as they feel the rope tighten; they give up trying to move.

Let's look at people. Take third-world countries. It is not starvation that kills the multitude. What kills people is dysentery that comes from the dung in the streets. The disease is infectious and will literally wipe out villages. That's what many recovery people—well, people in general—do. They hold onto the dung of their past, and it will kill them or destroy the life they could have. Let it go and give it to God.

Just a little side note. Another name of satan is Beelzebub or translated as King of the Dung. He is appropriately named the dung god (Strong 954).

The apostle Paul (Saul) who wrote more than 60 percent of the New Testament and who was also responsible for the killing and persecution of Christians, I believe, reflects the way people think. He had issues and thought he was doing right for God. In Romans, see what Saint Paul has to say after he was saved on the road to Damascus:

> "For I do not understand my own actions (I am baffled, bewildered).
> I do not practice or accomplish what I wish, but I do the very thing
> that I loathe (which my moral instinct condemns). For I know that
> nothing good dwells within me, that is, in my flesh. I can will what
> is right, but I cannot perform it. (I have the intention and urge to do
> what is right, but no power to carry it out). For I fail to practice the
> good deeds I desire to do, but the evil deeds that I do not desire to do
> are what I am (ever) doing." (Rom 7:15-19 Amp)

Remind you of anyone? And he goes on to say:

> ". . . but this one thing I do, forgetting those things which are behind,
> and reaching forth unto those things which are before." (Phil 3:13)

He totally forgot that Stephen, the church's first martyr—clothes were laid at his feet. He says he never hurt anyone. How can he say this? I wonder if he made amends? I also want to know who am I to judge another's servant? Paul is responsible for Paul's actions. We are not Paul. He forgot the things of the past, and if he can do it with his previous actions, then I can do it with the little squabbles I have in my life. If you read about the beatings he received, I think you will find that he suffered plenty or paid the consequences of his behaviors.

We are all a new creation. Thank God. Old things have passed away. All things are new. You are new. I am new. Make a mistake, start over right this minute. His mercies are new each morning. Acknowledge it and move on. Paul says the only thing he does right is to forget the past. What a lesson. If I could only realize who I really am and what I really mean to God, then I would never waste a second in condemnation of myself or others. Angels are not even permitted to tattle on you in heaven. Remind yourself of who you actually are to God.

> "What is man, that thou (God) art mindful of him? And the son of (earthborn) man, that You care for him? Yet you have made him but a little lower than God, and You have crowned him with glory and honor. You have made him to have dominion over the works of Your hands; You have put all things under his feet:" (Psalms 8: 4-6 Amp)

So that is who you are! You must be something very great and special to God that He is mindful of you and has crowned us (kings are crowned) with glory and honor. Oh how He loves us. Do you ever think of your children? I do all the time. Some Bibles state a little lower than angels. This is an incorrect translation as the actual word *Elohim*, for God, can be also translated angels but it should not be in this case. We are correctly translated a little lower than God.

Right now, right this very second He loves you and me. We do not live in the past. We live in the present. Not in tomorrow or yesterday. One day at a time is our motto. We acknowledge and ask to be forgiven if we have harmed others and we forgive others if they have harmed us, even if they did not deserve it. For their sake and ours! We need the light of God and want nothing to block His grace. We are in right standing. Always! His grace is upon us always and is conditional to our heart believing and not Him giving.

Fear

Are you living in fear? Well you can unless you are a new creation. You are now protected in the secret place of the Most High and His angels will be given charge over you. You are one of His. Remind Him. He wants you to! He even tells us to plead (not beg) with Him (Isa 43:26). And then the 91ST Psalm:

> " . . . For he shall give his angels charge over thee, to keep thee in all thy ways". (Psalm 91:11)

So why worry? God has not given us the spirit of fear but of power, and of love, and of a sound mind (2 Timothy 1:7). So if God did not give fear to you, who did? The one who steals, kills and destroys. Even Wilson told us that fear ought to be classified with stealing (Big Book 68). He knew how satan wants to distract us from God and His presence.

Praise God! You are on the right track, God's track. You must have it or the author of confusion and hurt would not be coming to attack you. If you do not think this is true, consider what Peter tells us:

> "Humble yourselves therefore under the mighty hand of God, that he may exalt you in due time: Casting all your care upon him: for he careth for you. Be sober, be vigilant; because *YOUR adversary the devil*, as a roaring lion, walketh about, seeking whom he may devour:" (Peter 5:6-8 emphasis added)

Peter knew. He learned from Jesus. Many times people seem to come against you. It is not the people. It is the evil one who uses people to come against us. We do not recognize who is behind them suggesting thoughts that push their and our buttons. And that is all the power the devil really has. He can push buttons and this is only to the extent that we allow him. He sometimes reminds me of our blessed teenagers. So many buttons to push and so little time.

All power and authority was taken from satan when Jesus overcame death and ascended into heaven. The physical earth is the devil's kingdom, but unfortunately for him, we live here. We belong to and are in God's kingdom. We gave our lives to God, and we are now with Him at the right hand of the Father.

This is also why we stay in conflict and are not peaceful. We have one foot in God's kingdom and try to keep one in this world. We cannot do it. We will fall. Get both feet where they belong. Half measures availed us nothing; we stood at the turning point and asked His protection and complete care with complete abandon (Big Book 59).

XI

THE POWER

There are two questions that I want to ask when I first meet someone in the fellowship, but I end up minding my own business. First, I want to know the length of their sobriety, and then find out if they use the power. The Big Book tells us:

> "Lack of power, that was our dilemma. We had to find a power greater than ourselves by which we could live, and it had to be a *Power greater than ourselves.* Obviously. But where and how were we to find this Power? Well, that's exactly what this book is about. Its main object is to enable you to find a Power greater than yourself which will solve your problem." (Big Book 45)

Now my sponsor always would tell me that the problem was me. Of course, he was telling me to look in the mirror and I would see the problem. So kind and gentle. Then he would tell me that he hoped I would find a greater power. He also told me that my stubbornness and self-will would only take me so far and that God would not interfere. He said God would let me do what I wanted without His help. So if God's power is the solution, where is this power and how do I get more?

> "Finally, my brethren, be strong in the Lord, and in the power of His might." (Eph 6:10)

I do not need to have the power in my own abilities. I just need to rely on His power. Jesus did not have the power when He came here to earth. Jesus was 100 percent God who had stripped Himself of all glory and honor. He was also 100 percent man who did not sin and fought the same fights and temptations that we do.

If He did not strip Himself of His authority and power, you and I could not identify with Him and His walk here on earth. He would not be a good role model because as you and I both know, it's easy to fall short. We would always being saying, "Yeah, *but*, He was God, I am man, and how can you expect me to be like Him"?

To make a stronger point, Jesus did not perform any miracles or mighty works here on earth until He was baptized by the Holy Spirit and received power from on High. He did not have the power in His human condition.

> "And the Holy Ghost descended in a bodily shape like a dove upon Him, and a voice came from heaven, which said, Thou art my beloved Son; in thee I am well pleased." (Luke 3:22)

Jesus, who was God and man, needed power from God, so you and I also need the same power that Jesus had. And guess what the first documented miracle He performed was? He turned water into wine (Jn 2:1). And you think He does not like drunks? How did we miss that party?

And the disciples also needed this power and were told in the book of Acts:

> "But you shall receive power (ability, efficiency, and might) when the Holy Spirit has come upon you, and you shall be My witnesses in Jerusalem and all Judea and Samaria and to the ends (the very bounds) of the earth". (Acts 1:8 Amp)

Who Is the Power?

Everyone who believes that Christ died on the cross and rose again for their salvation has received the Holy Spirit (or the power) in them. Jesus said:

> "But whosoever drinketh of the water that I shall give him shall never thirst; but the water that I shall give him shall be in him a well of water springing up into everlasting life." (John 4:14)

Water in this passage represents the Holy Spirit in the same way that oil, fire and a dove are examples in other verses. Jesus will give us the Holy Spirit, who will come and make His abode in us, once we believe. He says it shall be in us as a well.

A well is used for your own personal needs. Jesus says we have the Holy Spirit in us for our own needs and all that we must do is drink (actually believe) to receive it.

As a result of His indwelling, we now have the fruits of the Spirit sealed in our spirit (heart) along with our salvation and everything we need to live the abundant life. It is a large deposit for us to draw on. Here is a list of the fruits of the Spirit:

> "But the fruit of the Spirit is *love, joy, peace, longsuffering, gentleness, goodness, faith, meekness, temperance*: against such there is no law." (Gal 5:22-23 emphasis added)

But exactly how is this done? I thought that it is God who lives in me? Well, He does. We refer to it as the Trinity. Back in Genesis when God created man, He said, "Let *us* make man in *our* image and likeness." The *us* is: God who is in heaven, Jesus who is seated at His right side in heaven and the Holy Spirit who is here on earth. God is not here with us but His Spirit is. It is the Holy Spirit who carries out the work of God:

> "The earth was without form and an empty waste, and darkness was upon the face of the very great deep. The *Spirit of God was moving (hovering, brooding) over the face of the waters.* And God said, let there be light; and there was light." (Gen 1:2-3 Amp. emphasis added)

The Holy Spirit was moving back and forth waiting for the order from headquarters so that He could do what God told Him to do. And He did, "and there was light." The Holy Spirit created the light. So the Holy Spirit does only what the Father tells Him to do. The same as Jesus did only what the Father told Him to do. It is God's power that operates in us through the Holy Spirit when we ask in Jesus's name. We always pray to the Father, in the name of Jesus, and it is the Holy Spirit who carries out the task and provides the answers and power.

The Comforter

A man's last words are usually important. You will find Jesus's last words to be comforting. They start in John 13. In John 16:7, Jesus said:

> "Nevertheless I tell you the truth; it is *expedient* for you that I go away: for if I go not away, the Comforter will not come unto you; but if I depart, I will send him unto you." (emphasis added)

Jesus tells us that it is for our benefit that He left so that He could send us the Comforter. This is because Jesus Christ, the physical man, could be at only one place at one time, but the Holy Spirit, who is God, can be in many places at the same time. He tells us further who the Comforter is:

"And I will pray the Father, and he shall give you another *Comforter, (Counselor, Helper, Intercessor, Advocate, Strengthener, and Standby)* that he may remain with you forever; The Spirit of Truth, Whom the world cannot receive (welcome, take to its heart) because it does not see Him or know and recognize Him. But you know and recognize Him for He lives with you (constantly) and will be in you." (Jn 14:16-17 Amp. emphasis added)

So it is the Holy Spirit's responsibility to be all of the above plus what we find in other scriptures that you can look up. Here are some key findings:

- o He shows us the things that are freely given to us. (1 Cor 2:12-13)
- o He gives us wisdom and knowledge. (1 Cor 12:8)
- o He leads us. (Rom 8:14)
- o He guides us into all truth and shows us things to come. (John 16:13)
- o He separates us for the work that God calls us to. (Acts 13:2)
- o He forbids us to preach the Word at certain times and places. (Acts 16:6)
- o He commands and appoints. (Acts 8:29)
- o He makes us overseers. (Acts 20:28)
- o He sets us and the church. (1 Cor 12:28) (Meaning that it is God who establishes the different churches or denominations, and we should be less critical of others lest we believe God is in error.)
- o He makes us free from the law of sin and death. (Rom 8:2)
- o He allows us to enter into the kingdom of heaven. (John 3:3-5)
- o He renews us. (Titus 3:5)
- o He lives in us. (1 Cor 6:19)
- o He fills us. (Acts 2:4)
- o He makes us drunk. (Eph 5:18) (That's in the spirit, not with wine.)
- o He seals us. (Eph 1:13)
- o He gives us a security deposit that we will have eternal life. (2 Cor 1:22)

- ○ He anoints us and through Him we know all things. (2 John 2:20)
- ○ He anoints us to preach the gospel, heal the broken hearted, deliver the captives, give sight to the blind, set at liberty them that are bruised. (Luke 4:18)
- ○ He will teach us all things and bring all things to our remembrance. (John 14:26)
- ○ He empowers us. (Gal 5:16)

As you can see the Holy Spirit wears many hats to serve you and me. He can do only what our Father tells Him to do. Look up the listed verses for yourself, and prove them as He leads you and you seek Him.

Gifts of the Spirit

Along with the fruit of the Spirit, we are also given the gifts of the Spirit. Again, these are given to everyone who believes. Here is a partial listing of nine of these gifts:

> "But the manifestation of the Spirit is given to every man to profit withal. For to one is given by the Spirit *the word of wisdom*; to another the *word of knowledge* by the same Spirit; To another *faith* by the same Spirit; to another the *gifts of healing* by the same Spirit; to another the *working of miracles;* to another *prophecy*; to another *discerning of spirits*; to another *divers kinds of tongues*; to another the *interpretation of tongues*: (1 Cor 12:7-10 emphasis added)

And my favorite gift to seek is that of charity or the love that Paul tells us to seek first in 1 Corinthians 13:1. If you want something to happen, act in love.

But notice that these gifts are given to profit withal, meaning for the good and profit of others. We are well aware in the program that the only way you keep anything is by giving it away. So we seek these gifts to help others in life. We also know that by doing so, God will not be outdone. I think it's one of His favorite games. He always "one ups you". I hear Him saying, "You show me what you can do, and then I'll show you what I will do". That's His nature.

A Further In-Filling

There is a further in-filling of the Holy Spirit that is available to those who believe. It is above and beyond the indwelling that occurs naturally when you accept Christ. It is known as the Baptism of the Holy Spirit. Jesus said that His Father will give us the Holy Spirit if we ask. So we need to ask.

> "If ye then, being evil, know how to give good gifts unto your children; how much more shall your heavenly Father give the Holy Spirit to them that ask him?" (Luke 11:13)

This will equip you to help others as stated in John 7.

> "He that believeth on me, as the scripture hath said, out of his belly shall flow rivers of living water." (But this he spake of the Spirit, which they that believed on him should receive: for the Holy Ghost was not yet given; because that Jesus was not yet glorified.) (John 7:38-39)

Notice that Jesus is again speaking of the Holy Spirit. This time, however, He states rivers of living water for you and others which is contrasted against the well from John 4 that is for your personal consumption.

It is God's desire that we have and use the Holy Spirit who will manifest God's power here on earth for us and others.

XII

A NEW LIGHT

There has been much information provided here that will, as Wilson states, rocket you into another dimension. This dimension contains the power that you need to live in the abundant life that Jesus spoke about in the gospels.

Please do not believe that all we know is all there is. God has so much He wants to show us.

Find yourself a church. Attend one church that will fill you with and teach you the Word of God. The Word will bring life to you and is medicine to your soul. I have given many scriptures. Meditate on them. This will make an effective and long-lasting change in your life.

It is impossible for us, with our own self-will, to be made complete, bring about change or remove our shortcomings and character defects for any length of time in all areas of life. I should say that I have never been able to change myself by my willpower for any length of time, and this inability has caused many feelings of regret, fear and failure.

The only way to bring about results is by continuously being "being filled" with the Holy Spirit. In other words, you alone cannot quit doing and thinking about all the actions that you do not like about yourself by yourself. You must rely on God and allow your weaknesses to find your strength in Him. He confounds the strong with the foolish.

If you study the Word, you will find that God loves you just as you are and not as you *should* be. So why sweat it?

This understanding will create a new view of working the steps. When you surrender your life to God the way the Oxford Group teaches and the way Dr. Bob and Bill did, you come to believe that you are in right standing with your Father-God. You will be filled with the knowledge of His love for you. You will know that sin is no longer an issue with God and because you are right with God, you are right. With God there is now no condemnation for all of our stunts. Others maybe, but not God! We make other relationships right in the amends steps 8 and 9.

Many people struggle unnecessarily with the 4th step, taking a personal inventory. They do not understand the 3rd. They really believe that step 4 is confession, listing all of the wrongs and sins they committed. They believe this because we, as sponsors, did not really understand and did not explain the surrender part of step 3 to the newcomer. This moves the focus from looking at the sin to revealing the underlying traits in their personality that caused inappropriate thoughts and behaviors. The sin issue is removed in the step 3. Step 4 now has a totally new meaning and allows the person to see how fear and hurt have driven behavior for so many years. This is exactly why Wilson calls it an *inventory* rather than a *confession* and explains how to complete the process when you read it in the Big Book.

Similar issues now occur with steps 6 and 7, asking God to remove your shortcomings. First, when you become a new creation, old things pass away and all things are new. As a result of step 3 you no longer want to do the things you were doing. You cannot because God has now planted His law in your heart. If behaviors are driving you, you won't be doing them for long. If you are struggling, ask for God's wisdom as to the root cause and seek His power. Remember, we are created in His image, which is love. We are moving toward being total love. It's usually fear and hurt that keep us from getting there.

Because being filled with the Holy Spirit is the only way you can make effective long-lasting change, it now becomes God's problem, not yours. Ask to be filled to the top. Our only part is to believe, ask and wait. We give it to Him to work out in His time, and we now listen and continue seeking to know God. Our focus should be on finding out more of God's secrets and not on our defects. God made us, and it's His job.

> "For (of course) every house is built and furnished by someone, but the Builder of all things and the furnisher (of the entire equipment of all things) is God." (Heb 3:4 Amp)

So it is up to God and not us to bring about change and to furnish us. We lean on Him with our entire personality. That is why Jesus says, "The meek shall inherit the earth." Do not force anything. God will bring about what's needed in you, His way, and it will be better than you could have planned or desired on your own. You need only to ask.

Seek Further

These teachings are not difficult. We live in a technology era. Find creditable teachings on the Internet. Ask friends in and out of the program whom you consider spiritual how they learned about God. Take a course where they teach the Bible. Seek your pastor or minister at church for additional information. Get his views and prove them with scripture. If they don't prove out, then mediate on them before moving on. There are many avenues available if you honestly seek God as Wilson instructed us.

12 STEPS OF ALCOHOLICS ANONYMOUS

1. We admitted we were powerless over alcohol—that our lives had become unmanageable.
2. Came to believe that a power greater than ourselves could restore us to sanity.
3. Made a decision to turn our wills and our lives over to the care of God as we understood Him.
4. Made a searching and fearless moral inventory of ourselves.
5. Admitted to God, to ourselves, and to another human being the exact nature of our wrongs.
6. Were entirely ready to have God remove all these defects of character.
7. Humbly asked Him to remove our shortcomings.
8. Made a list of all persons we had harmed, and became willing to make amends to them all.
9. Made direct amends to such people wherever possible, except when to do so would injure them or others.
10. Continued to take personal inventory, and when we were wrong, promptly admitted it.
11. Sought through prayer and meditation to improve our conscious contact with God as we understood Him, praying only for knowledge of His will for us and the power to carry that out.
12. Having had a spiritual awakening as the result of these steps, we tried to carry this message to alcoholics, and to practice these principals in all our affairs.

END NOTES

Introduction

1. The Big Book is commonly said to have been authored by the first one hundred men and women of Alcoholics Anonymous. Alcoholics Anonymous's co-founder, Bill Wilson, was the primary writer and his text was reviewed by members in both the Akron and New York areas. Wilson tried to juggle the wording between born-again Christians, those who were open to God and the so-called atheists and agnostics.

    Page numbers are referenced to the 2nd and 3rd editions of the Big Book.

I. Alcoholics Anonymous and Religion

2. Dr. William D. Silkworth was a physician who practiced at Towns Hospital in New York. He tried repeatedly to free Bill Wilson of his alcoholism and was a staunch supporter of Wilson and Alcoholics Anonymous. He is the author of the letter found in the Big Book titled "The Doctor's Opinion."
3. Reverend Sam Shoemaker was Frank Buchman's right-hand man in the United States until their falling-out. He oversaw New York's Oxford Group that was responsible for sobering Rowland, Shep and Ebby, Bill's sponsor, who brought the message to Wilson. Shoemaker left New York in 1952 and pastored in Pittsburgh, Pennsylvania, before his death in 1963. There is an archive of Shoemaker's sermons, writings and teachings available in the Calvary Church in the East Liberty section of Pittsburgh.

V. Faith

4. Clarence Snyder was from Cleveland, Ohio, and become sober with the Oxford Group in Akron. He always claimed that he broke away from the Oxford Group first. This is untrue as Wilson had a falling-out with Shoemaker in 1937 and took

the meetings into Stepping Stones. In 1942 Wilson and Shoemaker rekindled their relationship and Wilson began giving credit to Shoemaker for his contributions.

5. We do not necessarily want an AA meeting to become a church meeting. There is strength and life if we could somehow intertwine the message of our experience, strength and hope along with biblical teachings.

6. Matthew 5 is the start of the Sermon on the Mount.

7. John 13 starts Jesus's final words to us before He was crucified. Here He tells about how He will not leave us alone and will send the Holy Spirit in his place. Other names for the Holy Spirit are Comforter, Counselor, Helper, Intercessor, Advocate, Strengthener and Standby, and He is exactly like Jesus.

8. Acts 2, 8, 9, 10, and 19 tells us how the people were further filled with the Holy Spirit. The Holy Spirit makes His dwelling in you at the new birth or when you turn away from old behaviors and accept Jesus as your Lord and Savior.

Being filled or baptized with the Holy Spirit is a further filling and is a separate experience, distinctive in itself, and is where we find the power to help others. Everyone is called to this filling.

9. Wilson experienced what we commonly call today an "open vision." This vision left him in a very peaceful place, and his mental obsession and physical compulsion for alcohol was lifted. As a result he pushed this need of a dramatic spiritual experience during the first six months of his recovery, and it did not work. This spectacular experience seldom occurs in most people, and when it does it generally precedes a trying time where the experience keeps you going. It is best not to seek this experience.

10. The whole idea of a necessary spiritual conversion was generated by the psychiatrist Carl Jung when he treated Rowland Hazzard in 1931. Hazzard brought this idea back to Wilson through Wilson's sponsor, Ebby. A conversion, like a spiritual experience, is necessary, but most people recognize it through hindsight. Seldom do you realize you changed until down the road.

11. I sometimes wonder if Bill actually understood and had the revelation that it is by God's grace that you are saved by the use of faith (or what you choose to believe). It is a revelation that must occur in your spirit. Like most gifts of God, you must seek it. I also personally have come to believe that you cannot break the bubble, so to speak, of grace. God's forgiveness is complete in and of itself and He no longer sees us in the same light in which we judge ourselves. It would also be foolish for us to want to try to break the bubble of grace.

VI. Seeking Recovery

12. Wilson later said that there were six original steps of the Oxford Group that were practice by the alcoholic as he entered into the group. These later statements are not consistent with what both he and Clarence Snyder verbally state in their leads of there being only 4 as recounted in this text. These 4 steps are found in the experiences recorded from early members. The confusion here comes when you consider the Oxford Group's five Cs (Kurtz 49). Early AA members were familiar with these and probably practiced them, but they do not lend themselves easily to AA's recovery program.

BIBLE VERSES

Introduction

1. *1 John 1:5* . . . Then this is the message that we have heard of him, and declare unto you, that God is light, and in him is no darkness at all.
2. *1 Thes 5:21* . . . Prove all things; hold fast that which is good.

I. Alcoholics Anonymous and Religion

3. *Deut 30:19* . . . I call heaven and earth to record this day against you, that I have set before you life and death, blessing and cursing: therefore choose life, that both thou and thy seed may live:

II. Spirit, Soul and Body

4. *Rom 1:18-20* . . . For the wrath of God is revealed from heaven against all ungodliness and unrighteousness of men, who hold the truth in righteousness; Because that which may be known of God is manifest in them; for God hath shewed it unto them. For the invisible things of him from the creation of the world are clearly seen, being understood by the things that are made, even his eternal power and Godhead; so that they are without excuse:
5. *Gen 1:26* . . . And God said, Let us make man in our image, after our likeness: and let them have dominion over the fish of the sea, and over the fowl of the air, and over the cattle, and over all the earth, and over every creeping thing that creepeth upon the earth.

III. Limiting God

6. *Acts 10:34* . . . Then Peter opened his mouth, and said, of a truth I perceive that God is no respecter of persons:
7. *Rom 2:11* . . . For there is no respect of persons with God.
8. *Col 3:25* . . . But he that doeth wrong shall receive for the wrong which he hath done: and there is no respect of persons. (This is saying God is just and doesn't play favorites so do not start feeling condemned.)
9. *Eph 1:19* . . . And what is the exceeding greatness of the power to us-ward who believes according to the working of his mighty power.
10. *Luke 10:19* . . . Behold, I give unto you power to tread on serpents and scorpions, and over all power of the enemy: and nothing shall by any means hurt you.
11. *Mt 16:19* . . . And I will give unto thee the keys of the kingdom of heaven: and whatsoever thou shall bind on earth shall be bound in heaven: and whatsoever thou shall loose on earth shall be loosed in heaven.
12. *Ps 115:16* . . . The heaven, even the heavens, are the Lord's: but the earth hath he given to the children of men.
13. *Col 2:9-10* . . . For in him dwelleth all the fullness of the Godhead bodily. And ye are complete in him, which is the head of all principality and power:
14. *Mt 28:18* . . . And Jesus came and spake unto them, saying. All power is given unto me in heaven and in earth. (We are His body and He is the head; therefore, we have all power.)
15. *Jn 14:12* . . . Verily, verily, I say unto you, He that believeth on me, the works that I do shall he do also; and greater works than these shall he do; because I go unto my Father.
16. *1 Cor 2:5* . . . That your faith shall not stand in the wisdom of men but in the power of God.
17. *2 Pet 3:9* . . . The Lord is not slack concerning his promises, as some men count slackness; but is long suffering to us-ward, not willing that any should perish, but that all should come to repentance.

IV. What the Old Timers Had

18. *1 Jn 4:21* . . . And this commandment have we from him, That he who loveth God love his brother also.
19. *1 Cor 13:1* . . . Though I speak with the tongues of men and of angels, and have not charity, I am become as sounding brass, or a tinkling cymbal.

20. *Rev 4:11* . . . Thou art worthy, O Lord, to receive glory and honour and power: for thou hast created all things, and for thy pleasure they are and were created.

21. *1 Jn 4:18* . . . There is no fear in love; but perfect love casteth out fear: because fear hath torment. He that feareth is not made perfect in love.

V. Faith

22. *Eph 2:8-9* . . . For by grace are ye saved through faith; and that not of yourselves: it is the gift of God: Not of works, lest any man should boast.

23. *Mt 6:7* . . . But when ye pray, use not vain repetitions, as the heathen do: for they think that they shall be heard for their much speaking.

24. *Eph 1:17-23* . . . That the God of our Lord Jesus Christ, the Father of glory, may give unto you the spirit of wisdom and revelation in the knowledge of him: the eyes of your understanding be enlightened; that ye may know what is the hope of his calling, and what the riches of the glory of the inheritance in the saints, And what is the exceeding greatness of his power to us-ward who believed according to the working of his power, which he wrought in Christ, when he raised him from the dead, and set him at his own right hand in the heavenly places, Far above all principality, and power, and might, and dominion, and every name that is named, not only in this world, but also in that which is to come: And hath put all things under his feet, and gave him to be the head over all things to the church, Which is the body, the fullness of him that filleth all in all.

25. *Eph 3:14-21* . . . For this cause I bow my knee to the Father of our Lord Jesus Christ, Of whom the whole family in heaven and earth is named, That he would grant you, according to the riches of his glory, to be strengthened with might by his Spirit in the inner man; That Christ may dwell in your hearts by faith; that ye being rooted and grounded in love, May be able to comprehend with all the saints what is the breadth, and length, and depth, and height; And to know the love of Christ, which passeth knowledge, that ye might be filled with all the fullness of God. Now unto him that is able to do exceedingly abundantly above all that we ask or think, according to the power that worketh in us, Unto him be glory in the church by Christ Jesus throughout all ages, world without end. Amen.

VI. Seeking Recovery

26. *John 10:10* . . . The thief cometh not, but for to steal, and to kill, and to destroy: I am come that they might have life, and that they might have it more abundantly.
27. *Heb 12:6* . . . But without faith it is impossible to please him: for he that cometh to God must believe that he is, and that he is a rewarder of them that diligently seek him.

VII. Early Steps in Recovery

28. *2 Cor 4:16* . . . For which cause we faint not; but though our outward man perish, yet the inward man is renewed day by day.
29. *Mat 6:34* . . . Take therefore no thought for the morrow: for the morrow shall take thought for the things of itself. Sufficient unto the day is the evil thereof.
30. *James 1:2* . . . My brethren, count it all joy when ye fall into divers temptations; (note: we must be able to do this because it would not be right for God to instruct us to do something that we could not do)
31. *Deut 28:1-15* . . . . In Gal 3:13 we learn that Christ has removed the curses of the law and we are left with the blessing. The following blessings are yours as a believer.

    [1]IF YOU will listen diligently to the voice of the Lord your God, being watchful to do all His commandments which I command you this day, the Lord your God will set you high above all the nations of the earth. [2]And all these blessings shall come upon you and overtake you if you heed the voice of the Lord your God. [3]Blessed shall you be in the city and blessed shall you be in the field. [4]Blessed shall be the fruit of your body and the fruit of your ground and the fruit of your beasts, the increase of your cattle and the young of your flock. [5]Blessed shall be your basket and your kneading trough. [6]Blessed shall you be when you come in and blessed shall you be when you go out. [7]The Lord shall cause your enemies who rise up against you to be defeated before your face; they shall come out against you one way and flee before you seven ways. [8]The Lord shall command the blessing upon you in your storehouse and in all that you undertake. And He will bless you in the land which the Lord your God gives you. [9]The Lord will establish you as a people holy to Himself, as He has sworn to you,

if you keep the commandments of the Lord your God and walk in His ways. [10]And all people of the earth shall see that you are called by the name [and in the presence of] the Lord, and they shall be afraid of you. [11]And the Lord shall make you have a surplus of prosperity, through the fruit of your body, of your livestock, and of your ground, in the land which the Lord swore to your fathers to give you. [12]The Lord shall open to you His good treasury, the heavens, to give the rain of your land in its season and to bless all the work of your hands; and you shall lend to many nations, but you shall not borrow. [13]And the Lord shall make you the head, and not the tail; and you shall be above only, and you shall not be beneath, if you heed the commandments of the Lord your God which I command you this day and are watchful to do them. [14]And you shall not turn aside from any of the words which I command you this day, to the right hand or to the left, to go after other gods to serve them. [15]But if you will not obey the voice of the Lord your God, being watchful to do all His commandments and His statutes which I command you this day, then all these curses shall come upon you and overtake you: (continue reading if you would like to see what curses have been removed)

VIII. Right Standing and Righteousness

32. *2 Cor 5:21* . . . For he that made him to be sin for us, who knew no sin; that we might be made the righteousness of God in him.
33. *Isa 59:2* . . . But your iniquities have separated between you and your God, and you sins have hid his face from you, that he will not hear.
34. *2 Tim 2:19* . . . Nevertheless the foundation of God standing sure, having this seal . . . .
35. *Eph 4:30* . . . And grieve not the Holy Spirit of God, whereby ye are sealed unto the day of redemption.
36. *Eph 1:13* . . . In whom ye also trusted, after that ye heard the word of truth, the gospel of your salvation: in whom also after ye believed, ye were sealed with that Holy Spirit of promise.
37. *2 Cor 1:22* . . . Who hath also sealed us, and given the earnest of the Spirit in our hearts.
38. *1 Jn 2:1* . . . My little children, these things write I unto you, that ye sin not. And *if* any man sin, we have an advocate with the Father, Jesus Christ the righteous:

IX. Forgiveness and Forgetting

39. *1 Cor 14:33* . . . For God is not the author of confusion, but of peace, as in all churches of the saints.
40. *Isa 53:5* . . . But he was wounded for our transgressions, he was bruised for our iniquities, the chastisement of our peace was upon him; and with his stripes we are healed.

X. Living in the Present

41. *Isa 43:26* . . . Put me in remembrance: let us plead together: declare thou, that thou mayest be justified.
42. *2 Tim 1:7* . . . For God hath not given us the spirit of fear; but of power, and of love, and of a sound mind.

BIBLIOGRAPHY

B., Dick. *The Oxford Group & Alcoholics Anonymous.* Kihei, Maui, Hawaii: Paradise Research Publications, Inc., 1998.

Barger, Mel. *New Wine.* Center City, Minnesota: Hazelden Educational Materials, 1991.

Knippel, Charles. *Samuel Shoemaker's Theological Influence on William G. Wilson's Twelve Step Program of Recovery.* Ann Arbor, Michigan: UMI Dissertation Service, 1991.

Kurtz, Ernest. *Not God.* Center City, Minnesota: Hazelden Educational Materials, 1979.

Snyder, Clarence. *The History of AA from The Home Brewmeister.* Two-disc CD Recording, (date not given).

Strong, James. *Strong's Exhaustive Concordance of the Bible.* Peabody, Massachusetts: Hendrickson Publishers, (date not given).

Wilson, William. *Alcoholics Anonymous.* New York City, New York: Alcoholic Anonymous World Services, Inc., 1955 (2nd Edition).

Wilson, William. *Twelve Steps and Twelve Traditions.* New York City, New York: Alcoholic Anonymous World Services, Inc., 2007.

Wilson, William. *The Day Doctor Bob Died.* CD #1 recording of lead at Kip Bay Group, 1st Anniversary. (Nov 16, 1950).

Unless otherwise indicated, all scripture quotations are from the King James Version of the Bible.

Scripture references marked AMP are taken from the KJV Parallel Bible AMP. Copyright 1954, 1958, 1962, 1964, 1965, 1987 by The Lockman Foundation. Used by permission of Zondervan Publishing House. All rights reserved.

Charles Finney

D.L. Moody

Jessie Penn-Lewis

Frank Buchman

Sam Shoemaker

1st-Century Christian Fellowship

1926 Oxford Group

1941 Moral Re-Armament

1931- Carl Jung (conversion)

Rowland Hazzard

Ebby Thatcher
Shep Cornell

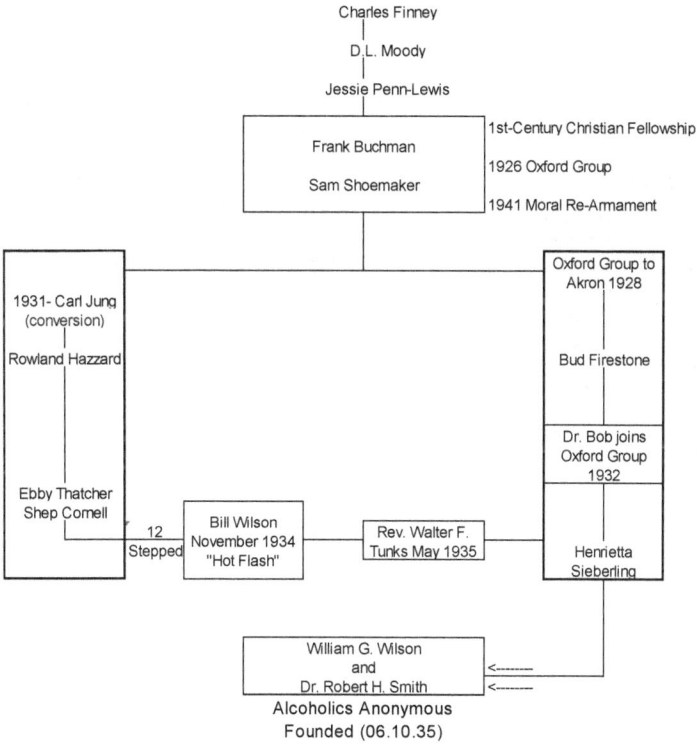

Oxford Group to Akron 1928

Bud Firestone

Dr. Bob joins Oxford Group 1932

12 Stepped

Bill Wilson
November 1934
"Hot Flash"

Rev. Walter F.
Tunks May 1935

Henrietta Sieberling

William G. Wilson
and
Dr. Robert H. Smith

Alcoholics Anonymous
Founded (06.10.35)

CPSIA information can be obtained
at www.ICGtesting.com
Printed in the USA
LVHW111430010719
622873LV00001B/291/P

9 781441 598790